JESUS AS TEACHER

Understanding Jesus Today

Edited by Howard Clark Kee

Growing interest in the historical Jesus can be frustrated by diverse and conflicting claims about what he said and did. This series brings together in accessible form the conclusions of an international team of distinguished scholars regarding various important aspects of Jesus' teaching. All of the authors have extensively analyzed the biblical and contextual evidence about who Jesus was and what he taught, and they summarize their findings here in easily readable and stimulating discussions. Each book includes questions for further thought and recommendations for further reading on the topic covered.

Other Books in the Series

Howard Clark Kee, *What Can We Know About Jesus?*
John Riches, *The World of Jesus: First Century Judaism in Crisis*
David Tiede, *Jesus and the Future*

Jesus as Teacher

PHEME PERKINS
Department of Theology, Boston College

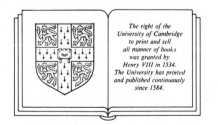

The right of the
University of Cambridge
to print and sell
all manner of books
was granted by
Henry VIII in 1534.
The University has printed
and published continuously
since 1584.

CAMBRIDGE UNIVERSITY PRESS

Cambridge
New York   Port Chester   Melbourne   Sydney

Published by the Press Syndicate of the University of Cambridge
The Pitt Building, Trumpington Street, Cambridge CB2 1RP
40 West 20th Street, New York, NY 10011, USA
10 Stamford Road, Oakleigh, Melbourne 3166, Australia

© Cambridge University Press 1990

First published 1990
Reprinted 1991 (twice)

Printed in the United States of America

Library of Congress Cataloging-in-Publication Data
Perkins, Pheme.
Jesus as Teacher / Pheme Perkins.
    p.   cm. – (Understanding Jesus today)
Includes bibliographical references.
ISBN 0–521–36624–0. – ISBN 0–521–36695–X (pbk.)
1. Jesus Christ – Teaching methods.   2. Jesus Christ – Teachings.
I. Title.   II. Series.
BT590.T5P475   1990
232.9'04—dc20   90–32437
                                                 CIP

British Library Cataloguing in Publication Data
Perkins, Pheme
Jesus as teacher.
1. Jesus Christ. Ministry
I. Title   II. Series
232.95

ISBN 0-521-36624-0 hardback
ISBN 0-521-36695-X paperback

Contents

Chapter 1

Teaching and Learning in Jesus' World

When we think of someone as a teacher, we usually think of that person as offering instruction in a school. Pupils are enrolled in the school and follow a system of education established by the school. There were some schools in Jesus' time that would fit this picture. Up until age twelve both boys and girls who lived in cities and towns spent their mornings in schools where they learned the basics of reading and writing. After that age, only boys of wealthier families continued their education. They were sent to teachers who drilled them in the classics, especially the epic poets Homer and Hesiod, and taught them how to speak like educated men. They would study and seek to imitate famous orators like Demosthenes. Rhetoric was the only training for government or public service. Young men learned the duties and behavior appropriate to various offices by imitating older men, especially natural or adoptive fathers and uncles. Sons of craftsmen learned their trade as apprentices. Schools did not train people for later life. Similarly the sons of priests learned what they needed to know for service in the Temple from their fathers.

Jesus, however, did not establish a school with a philosophical doctrine or special method of interpreting the Law. His followers learned by observing what he said and did in different situations. The Gospels refer to a group of Jesus' disciples as the twelve. Mark 3:14–19 pictures the twelve as having been selected from the larger number of followers. They are shown receiving special instruction from Jesus (Mk 4:10; 9:35; Mt 11:1). Jesus sends them to heal and to preach the Kingdom (Mk

1

3:13, 6:7; Mt 10:1; Lk 9:1–2) and promises them a place as leaders of the renewed Israel at the judgment (Mt 19:28; Lk 22:30).

Jesus' message to the crowds and his instruction to the disciples do not differ in content. The gospel writers even disagree over whether a particular teaching was spoken privately to the disciples or publicly to the crowds. For example, Mark 10:10–12 has Jesus teaching the disciples that whoever divorces his wife commits adultery against her, whereas Matthew 19:9 and 5:31–2 have this saying as public teaching.

In order to understand what the people who heard Jesus expected from his teaching, we need to know about the different types of teachers in the first century. We want to know what Jesus shares with other teachers as well as what was different about his teaching.

Writings of the period speak of four types of teachers who had adult followers: philosophers; sages; interpreters of the Jewish Law, scribes, and Pharisees; and prophets or seers. Our evidence for philosophers includes the writings of individual philosophers as well as biographical summaries of the opinions of various philosophers such as Diogenes Laertius' *History of Philosophy; or, On the Lives, Opinions, and Apothegms of Famous Philosophers* (first half of third century C.E.). A sage from Jerusalem, Yeshua ben Sira (early second century B.C.E.), collected wisdom sayings in a book that his grandson translated into Greek ca. 132 B.C.E. His work is included in the Old Testament apocrypha as Sirach or Ecclesiasticus. We do not possess any writings of the scribes and Pharisees whom we meet in the pages of the New Testament. However, their interpretations of the Law may be represented in later rabbinic collections of Jewish Law such as the Mishnah (ca. 200 C.E.). We do possess some direct examples of "scribal" interpretations of the Law from the sectarian Essene communities. The Essene writings found near the Dead Sea included rules governing life in Essene communities as well as other fragments of legal rulings. Prophets and seers generally did not leave written records. The New Testament preserves only a few words attributed to John the Baptist (Mk 1:7–8; Mt 3:7–10). The first-century Jewish historian Josephus (ca. 38–100 C.E.) describes a prophet, Joshua ben Ananiah, who predicted the destruction of Jerusalem from 62 C.E. until the city's destruction in the year 70 (*War* vi.300–9). He also reports that some Essenes studied the Hebrew prophets and were able to make accurate prophecies of their own (*War* ii.159). A Christian prophet, John (ca. 95 C.E.), cast his prophecies and visions in the form of a book, Revelation.

Philosopher-Teachers

Ancient philosophers were characterized as belonging to specific schools, that is, groups that held distinct doctrines and defended their positions against the views of the other schools. Most of the philosophers of Jesus' time traced their teaching to the founder of their particular school, who had lived as many as several centuries before. Sometimes the founder had created an institution with social or legal arrangements that gave it the appearance of a religious cult. Pythagoras (late sixth century B.C.E.) was said to have presided over a band of disciples who followed a way of life taught by the founder, including special dietary rules and sharing property in common. The original Pythagorean communities had disappeared by the fourth century B.C.E., but a Pythagorean revival began among Roman intellectuals in the first century B.C.E. A certain Nigidius Fugulus, who was praetor in 58 B.C.E., started an association in Rome.

Another Pythagorean, Apollonius of Tyana, a Greek city in Cappadocia, wandered about the empire teaching during the first century C.E. A biography of Apollonius was written for the empress Julia Domna in the early third century C.E. Its

author, Philostratus, says that miraculous signs, especially a
bolt of lightning suspended in the sky, accompanied Apollonius' birth (*Life* I.5). He pictured Apollonius preaching in
Babylon, India, and Egypt as well as in Rome and cities of Asia
Minor (e.g., Ephesus) and Greece. He confronted various rulers
by refusing to worship them as divine, nor would he engage in
their pursuits like hunting animals or indulge their demands to
use his miraculous powers for material advantage. He might
attempt to teach the king wisdom as when he refused to tor-
ture animals that the king kept in a royal park for hunting. The
king then challenged Apollonius by asking how he could secure his power. The philosopher responded, "By honouring
many and trusting few" (*Life* I.38). He cautioned the king of
Syria not to resist Roman power over a few small villages.
When the king became sick, Apollonius used philosophy to
teach him to be indifferent even to death. This biography is
often compared with the treatment of Jesus in the Gospels as
well as with stories told about the apostles. Apollonius is said
to have cured a young girl by touching her and whispering to
her (*Life* IV.45).

A philosophical school that endured for hundreds of years,
the Academy at Athens, passed down the teachings of its
founder, the philosopher Plato (fourth century B.C.E.). The
Academy, however, was legally constituted as a religious cult
devoted to the Muses. Socrates, Plato's teacher (who was executed by the Athenians in 399 B.C.E. for leading the young
astray and not venerating the traditional gods), and Plato were
the "heroes" venerated by the cult. The Academy continued to
be a school to which people came to learn philosophy until the
Roman emperor Justinian closed it in 529 C.E. A woman teacher at the Academy, Hypatia from Alexandria, was lynched by a
Christian mob in the year 415.

Epicurus (341–270 B.C.E.) may have been the first philosopher to found a school as an institution. Small groups of Epi-

cureans, who referred to themselves as "friends," met on the twentieth of each month to dine in honor of Epicurus. They reverenced their founder as a "god" by celebrating his birthday and by putting up icons and crypts bearing his image. Because they insisted that everything in the universe – even the gods – was composed of atoms (which they pictured as tiny, indivisible particles of different shapes) and the void (i.e., the empty space in which atoms move), and that the gods did not concern themselves with humans, Epicureans were often considered atheists. Because they thought that in order to live as pleasantly as possible, a person should avoid the turmoil of a public life, Epicureans were felt to be outsiders and were even condemned for "hatred of humanity."

The early Christians also formed small groups of "friends" who pursued a life of moral virtue taught by their founder and were encouraged to "live quietly" (1 Thes 4:11), not involving themselves in the affairs of their neighbors. As a result, they were sometimes thought to be like the Epicureans: atheists and haters of humanity.

The most influential philosophy among the educated classes of the Roman world was Stoicism. It was named for the colonnade or public porch, the painted Stoa in Athens, where its founder, Zeno (335–263 B.C.E.), taught. Stoics held that happiness could be achieved only through inner discipline. No one controls the things that happen to him or her in life. But if one overcomes human passions, then neither excessive evils nor excessive goods will upset one's happiness or moral character. Stoics often encouraged people to resist evils done by the emperors. As a result, the emperor Domitian (51–96 C.E.) banned philosophers from Rome in 92–94.

The Stoic quest for self-sufficiency as the key to happiness took its most radical form in the Cynics. "Cynic" is derived from the Greek word for "dog" and was used as a general term of scorn (as in Phil 3:2). The Cynics turned the scorn directed at them to their own advantage by claiming that they did indeed live like dogs. They rejected all the cultural trappings of home and family. They hardened themselves to live outdoors with rough clothing, which included a philosopher's cloak and staff, eating with minimal utensils whatever food could be scavenged. Cynics wandered from place to place and preached to anyone who would listen about the foolishness of all the things that cause most people anxiety. People think that they have to have clothes, children, friends, possessions, good food, and other nonessentials and so they wear themselves out trying to attain them. As people become more dependent on the luxuries of society, they also become physically and mentally weaker. They are no longer able to live naturally like the animals.

Some of the sayings of Jesus fit the mood of Cynical preaching. The anxieties of human life are to be met by looking at the natural clothing and food that God provides for plants and animals (Mt 6:25–32). The instructions to go and preach without taking any provisions for the journey (Mt 10:7–11) would have suggested to some of Matthew's readers that Jesus' disciples had adopted the life-style of wandering Cynics.

All types of philosophy called for a "conversion." Without philosophy, people lived lives that were caught in vice or foolishness. They had to exchange that way of living for a philosophical life of virtue. Sometimes philosophers even spoke of themselves as doctors for the human soul. Instead of the fleeting pleasures on which most people build their happiness, the philosopher promised a happiness that could not be taken away.

Sometimes devotion to philosophy also led to conflict with the rulers of society. The greatest philosopher-martyr was Socrates (d. 399 B.C.E.), who had neglected his trade and his family to go about Athens questioning its citizens about virtue. The Athenians put the elderly Socrates on trial for denying the gods worshiped by the city and for corrupting the youth with his teaching. His trial and heroic death – he engaged in philosophical conversation until the end – were immortalized in dialogues by one of those followers, Plato (see Plato's *Apology, Crito, Phaedo*). Other philosophers who challenged emperors and kings often looked back to the example of Socrates. The true philosopher had to demonstrate that his life matched his teaching even if it meant death.

Some scholars have even claimed to find influences from the Socrates story in Paul's defense of his apostolate in 2 Corinthians 10–13. Just as Socrates had condemned the Athenians for following teachers who demanded large fees, used impressive and flattering language, and had no real concern for making their pupils better, Paul claims that the "superapostles" who have turned the Corinthians against him because he does not demand money or use elaborate rhetoric are simply abusing the Corinthians for their own gain. The portrayal of Paul's imprisonment in 2 Timothy shows that the apostle was committed to the gospel even when some fellow Christians had abandoned him (cf. 2 Tm 1:8–18; 3:10–13; 4:9–18). Luke presents Jesus' death as a heroic example of his teaching. Jesus does not react to the hatred and scorn of his opponents but continues to offer God's forgiveness to those who repent (Lk 23:32–43). Such a death shows that Jesus is not the criminal he is accused of being, but is truly innocent (Lk 23:46–8).

Sages and Teachers of Wisdom

The philosopher-teachers originated in the Greek city-states. After Alexander's conquests in Asia Minor, the Middle East, and Egypt (336–23 B.C.E), Greek cities and their culture were spread throughout the region. Some Jews translated their Scriptures from Hebrew into Greek. Others began to write books to demonstrate the superiority of Judaism as a source of wisdom.

Some claimed that Moses and the prophets taught the Greek philosophers.

When a group of Jews hoping to turn Jerusalem into a city-state on the Greek model enlisted the aid of their Syrian ruler, Antiochus IV, a civil war broke out (166 B.C.E.). Resistance to such Hellenization, which included introducing pagan worship in the Temple, proved strong enough to expel the Syrians and their allies. For about a century – until it was conquered by Rome in 63 B.C.E. – Judea was an independent state.

Even though the Jews had defended their ancestral tradition from being collapsed into the general patterns of Hellenistic culture, they did not withdraw into a cultural ghetto. Jewish writers sought to show that their traditions were more ancient than the Greek traditions and consequently were better sources of wisdom and virtue. The Jewish community had its guide to a just way of life in the Law of Moses. Jews could also point to the wisdom attributed to wise men of the past. King Solomon was revered as a source of wisdom (1 Kgs 4:29–34). The Old Testament contains two books of wise sayings attributed to him, Proverbs and Ecclesiastes. Job is also a wisdom book. Other wisdom books were part of the Greek version of the Old Testament, Sirach (Ecclesiasticus) and Wisdom of Solomon.

Following the advice of the sage is supposed to bring success and happiness. The audience is exhorted to act patiently, be guarded in their speech, be honest in dealing with others, work hard, choose friends carefully and be loyal to them, and avoid vices such as greed, drunkenness, and laziness. Some traditions, like those in Proverbs, are optimistic about human behavior. Others like Ecclesiastes and Job insist that even the righteous person can expect evils and misfortunes.

Wisdom is often communicated in the form of admonitions from father to son. If the son follows the sage's advice, he will prosper and become a respected member of the community, perhaps even a counselor to kings. Many of the proverbs and sayings passed down in this way were probably part of the oral lore of the family or clan. Comparable examples can be found in Egyptian and Babylonian cultures. However, the special advice aimed at training courtiers probably stems from some form of school for scribes such as we find in Egypt and Babylon. Proverbs 22:17–24:22 contains close parallels to Egyptian wisdom teaching.

The young are often warned against the charms of women (Prv 2:16–19; 7:6–27; 8:13–18). If they are able to avoid the temptress and the foolish woman, they may be lucky enough to marry a woman of true virtue (Prv 31:10–31). Wisdom herself is pictured as a woman calling humanity. She provides those who hear her with understanding and virtue (Prv 8:1–21). Wisdom was the "first" of all creation and served as God's assistant in shaping the universe (Prv 8:22–31). She lays out a rich banquet in her temple for those who come to her (Prv 9:1–6).

Ecclesiasticus is an example of how the wisdom tradition was passed on within a family and at the same time adapted to new circumstances. Written by Yeshua ben Sira ("Jesus, the son of Sira") around 132 B.C.E., this wisdom book was translated into Greek by the author's grandson, who had moved to Alexandria, an Egyptian city with a large, Greek-speaking Jewish population. In some instances his translation sharpened the focus of an admonition so that its message challenged the ethical presuppositions of the Hellenistic world. Where ben Sira had "Do not mock at the poor person's life," his grandson translated, "Do not cheat a poor man of his livelihood" (Ecclus 4:1–3; 34:20–1). In the Hellenistic city a poor person had no "rights" as we understand the term. Without a rich relative or patron such a poor person could be abused by the legal process. Cities felt no obligation to provide for the needy. But our translator wants his readers to have no doubt about the message of the biblical tradition. God requires special concern for the poor. God will not show favoritism to one person over another but hears the victim of injustice, orphan, and widow (35:13–14).

Jewish tradition considered the Law of Moses a source of wisdom. Wisdom came to those who studied it and lived by its precepts. For the philosopher-teachers the life of the philosopher served as the lived example of a school's teaching. We find a parallel in the wisdom tradition's picture of the sage (see Ecclus 39:1–11).

Special virtues were associated with the patriarchs of the twelve tribes of Israel. Joseph was often held up as a model (read Gn 37:1–47:27). He is a wise courtier who overcame the evils his brothers and others brought upon him. His judicious administration saved the kingdom of Egypt and his family. Joseph's willingness to forgive the brothers who sold him into slavery was used by Jewish writers as an example of love of neighbor. Here is a description of Joseph from the Testament of Benjamin, a second-century B.C.E. writing:

You also, therefore my children, love the Lord God of heaven and earth and keep his commandments, following the example of the good and holy man Joseph. And let your mind be unto good, even as you know me, for he that has his mind right sees all things rightly. Fear the Lord and love your neighbor; and even though the spirits of Beliar [i.e., Satan] afflict you with every evil, yet they will not rule over you even as they did not rule Joseph, my brother. How many men wished to kill him, and God shielded him! For whoever fears God and loves his neighbor, cannot be struck by the spirit of Beliar, since that person is shielded by the fear of God. Nor can such persons be ruled over by means of humans or beasts, for they are helped by the Lord through the love which they have for their neighbors. (3:1–5)

Teachers of the Law: Scribes, Pharisees, and Rabbis

The Gospels frequently mention Pharisees and scribes as Jewish teachers (e.g., Mk 2:6, 26; 3:22; 7:1, 5). "Rabbi," another expression used as a title of respect for a teacher, is much less frequently encountered (cf. Mt 23:7; Jn 1:38). Occasionally a gospel writer has the people address Jesus as "rabbi" (Mt 26:49; Mk 9:5; 10:51; 11:21; Jn 1:49; 4:31; 6:25; 9:2; 11:8). Scribes, Pharisees, and rabbis were all engaged in interpreting the Jewish Law.

"Scribe" (or in Greek, *grammateus*) originally referred to court officials. The scribe with his writing slate is pictured in Egyptian art going back thousands of years. Originally scribes were those trained in the craft of writing. They were able to record the laws, economic transactions, and the complex diplomatic dealings of the king. They might also record the wisdom traditions that guided those who served at court. We read about scribes serving the Jewish kings in 2 Samuel 8:17 and 1 Kings 4:3.

After the Babylonian exile (587 B.C.E.), "scribe" takes on a new meaning and refers to persons with special learning in the Mosaic Law. This learning was prized by those who sought to reestablish the people of Israel on the basis of their ancestral traditions (Ezr 7:6, 11; Neh 8:1). During the second century B.C.E., scribes were part of the circle of priests and Levites trying to keep the people from taking on Greek customs. Their interpretations of the Law often insisted on ritual purity and separation from non-Jews. Other scribes may have been supporting those members of the temple priesthood and the Jerusalem aristocracy who went along with Greek customs.

Interpretation of the Law played a critical role in the social and political life of the Jewish people. While one group of scribes and Levites criticized the corruption of those who were trying to turn Jerusalem into a Greek city-state, another group took a more radical step. In the middle of the second century B.C.E., they separated from other Jews. We knew very little about this group, called "Essenes," until a library of Essene scrolls was discovered in the caves at Qumran. There, below the hills near the Dead Sea, archaeologists uncovered the remains of a monastic settlement. Inkwells and remains of long tables suggest that one of the rooms was used for copying the biblical scrolls, as well as for preparing books of community laws and liturgies, books of biblical interpretation, and the other writings that make up the library. In addition to the rules for those who lived in the desert settlement, other rules apply to groups of Essenes who lived in towns and villages. We do not know how large this movement of pious Jews was. However, archaeological remains show that the monastic community had to be refounded after an earthquake in 31 B.C.E. It then continued to exist until the Romans destroyed the settlement in 68 C.E.

Hints about the early history of the group are found in their interpretation of the prophets, but we cannot with any certainty attach the symbolic references to persons and events known to us from other sources. Prophetic texts were said to have predicted that their founder, known only as the Teacher of Righteousness, would withdraw to form a new covenant with God in the desert. They foretold the conflict between the Teacher and someone called the "Wicked Priest." The "Wicked Priest" even pursued the Teacher and his followers into the desert where he attacked them on a feast day.

Essenes felt that people whom they referred to as "interpreters of smooth things" and "teachers of lies" were leading other Jews astray. One of the longest scrolls, the Temple Scroll, published in 1977, gives the Essene prescription for purification and reconstruction of the Temple in Jerusalem. A new priesthood of unquestioned purity would be established. All the people would finally turn to obey God in complete holiness. This definition of holiness included avoiding persons, situations, and foods that made one "unclean" or "polluted" in God's eyes as well as a strict ethical code. Here is a passage from that scroll:

. . . . unclean . . . You shall not pollute yourselves with them. . . . And everyone who lifts from their bones or from their carcass skin, flesh or claws shall wash his clothes and bathe in water. And after the sun is set he is clean. So warn the Israelites against all the uncleanness. They shall not defile themselves with the things which I tell you on this mountain. For I, Yahweh, dwell among the Israelites; so make yourselves holy and be holy. . . . Appoint judges and officers for yourselves in all your gates so that they may judge the people with just judgment, and not accept bribes and not pervert justice. . . . Justice, justice you shall strive after so that you may live and inherit the land I give you as an inheritance forever. And the man who takes a bribe and perverts justice in judgment shall be killed, and you shall not be afraid of killing him. You shall not behave in your land as the Gentiles behave; in every place they are accustomed to sacrifice. . . . and place for themselves stone images to bow down before them. (Column 51)

Traditions of biblical interpretation and legal observance distinguished groups of Jews from one another. The expression "the pious" (hasidim) appears to have been used by some groups to describe their opposition to a lax interpretation of the Law that threatened the distinctiveness of Judaism. The Pharisees were a group of nonpriestly interpreters of the Law who also emerged from the hasidic movements of the second century B.C.E. The Greek name "Pharisee" appears to be taken from the Aramaic Perisaye, "separated ones." Perhaps it was originally a nickname pinned on the group by others who objected to their interpretation of the Torah.

The Pharisees insisted that the Law should be carefully observed. In addition to the written Law, they also appealed to a tradition of "oral Law," which they said had been handed down from Moses and the "elders." Mark 7:3 refers to traditions about washings before meals that the Pharisees observed. Although Jesus attacks this concern with food rules and purification rituals as missing the point of what God really asks of humans, the Pharisees were proud of the care with which they observed dietary and purity laws. They also called for careful observance of the Sabbath and other feast days.

For the Pharisees, study of the Law was even an act of worship. If they could spread knowledge of the Law among the people, Israel would become a holy people. Paul had been a Pharisee before he became a Christian. As we noted, in the New Testament "rabbi" occurs rarely. It seems to be a general word of respect for a teacher. However, after the Temple was destroyed in 70 C.E., the Pharisees became the leading teachers of Judaism. Without the Temple, the priests and Levites who carried out the rituals there had no function. The Essene community had been destroyed by the Roman army. The Romans, however, permitted some Pharisees to establish a school for the study of the Law. During this period "rabbi" came to be used for a person who was a teacher and interpreter of the Law. As the rabbinic tradition came to be written down between 70 and 200 C.E., a chain of teachers going back to the second century B.C.E. was created.

The most famous members of this chain were a pair of teachers known as Hillel and Shammai, both of whom lived at the end of the first century B.C.E. Each is said to have headed a school of Torah scholars. The two schools differed in details of interpretation. Hillel became known as milder than Shammai. A later legend said of Shammai that when his daughter-in-law had a son on the Feast of Tabernacles, Shammai had a hole made in the ceiling and the roof covered with branches so that the child would celebrate the feast as required by the Law.

Hillel is said to have been responsible for a ruling that appeared to contradict the Torah but which had important economic consequences. Deuteronomy 15:1–11 requires that all debts be forgiven every seven years. The result was that people were reluctant to lend money to others when a sabbatical year was likely to lead to cancellation of the debt. Economic factors such as trade and taxes collected in coin made loans a frequent necessity in the Roman period. Hillel solved the dilemma by introducing a judicial procedure called *prosbule,* which protected the creditor during the sabbatical year. The loan had to be made before a court with the following declaration: "I, [creditor's name], deliver to you, judges of [name of place], the declaration that I may demand payment of all my outstanding debts at any time I choose." An Aramaic loan document from 55/56 C.E. has the debtor promise repayment of a loan by a certain date. If the debtor defaults, a 20 percent penalty is added to the loan even if the loan falls due during a sabbatical year.

These examples show how important interpretation of the Law could be in everyday life. In order for a scribe, Pharisee, Essene, or rabbi to become a teacher of the Law, he would have to spend years studying the Law under a teacher. Young men would have to journey to the teacher and be accepted as his students. Acts 22:3 reports that Paul had gone to Jerusalem to study with one of the most famous teachers there, Gamaliel. Most people would never be able to study the Law under a famous teacher. Their knowledge of the Law came through the reading and interpretation that took place in the local synagogue on the Sabbath.

Jews pointed to this synagogue teaching with pride. Josephus commented that "he [Moses] made the Law to be an excellent and necessary subject of instruction in that it is not to be heard but once or twice or frequently, but he ordained that every week the people should set aside their other occupations and gather to listen to the Law and learn it accurately" (*Against Apion* ii.17 [175]). Philo (ca. 20 B.C.E.–50 C.E.), a Jewish philosopher whose allegorical interpretations of the Greek Old Testament sought to show that it contained philosophical wisdom, described the synagogues as schools that taught virtue and the "ancestral philosophy" (*Life of Moses* ii.39 [216]). For Philo, the Law provides all the people with a virtue the philosophers had taught only to the educated minority.

Prophets and Visionaries

As people began to make interpretation of the Law the center of Jewish life in the two or three centuries before Jesus, prophets as guides for the life of the nation appear less frequently. The last prophetic writings in the Old Testament, Haggai, Zechariah, and Malachi, are not later than the fifth century B.C.E. Scholars think that prophets may have continued to be minor functionaries attached to the Temple (see 1 Chr 25). Often scribes and Pharisees would use the writings of the prophets as examples of how the Law is to be interpreted. Matthew 5:17, for example, speaks of Jesus' teaching "fulfilling the Law and the prophets." The Hebrew prophets had often called the people to repentance. They had insisted that the injustice, idolatry, and evils of the nation were breaking the bond that God established with the people through Moses. Deuteronomy 18:18–19 promises that God will raise up another prophet like Moses to lead the people. In Jesus' day, some groups like the Essenes were hoping to see that Mosaic prophet appear together with a true Davidic king and a true priest. But until these "messianic" figures came, the people were to be guided by those who interpreted the Law.

Interpreters of the Law could not fulfill the functions of prophets. They could not speak a word of warning to the nation. They could not point to new manifestations of God's power of judgment in the future, nor could they call rulers or priests to answer for conduct that went against the will of God. Prophecy provides insights into the actions and judgments of God.

Persons spoke and wrote prophetic words about their own time. Some continued along the lines established by the Old Testament prophets. But we also find a new type of writing known as "apocalyptic" (from the Greek word for "revelation") writing, which many scholars think began as early as the third century B.C.E. Often presented as the visions of a past figure like Adam, Enoch, Moses, Abraham, Daniel, or Ezra, these apocalyptic writings look to a future in which God will overthrow the evils of the world and establish a new kingdom of righteousness.

Some include visions of heavenly regions that the seer or prophet had visited along with oracles of the future learned from angels. Others look down through the future history of Israel to the end time. The prophecies contained in these writings often draw on complex symbolism with roots in ancient mythology, earlier biblical writings, wisdom traditions, and the like. Therefore many scholars think of apocalyptic works as the result of study and reinterpretation of earlier traditions. The Book of Daniel refers to "the wise" who instruct the people (11:33, 35). Apocalyptic prophecy may have been learned in groups of teachers and followers.

The symbolic character of apocalyptic writing also suggests that apocalyptic prophets limited their teaching to groups of like-minded sympathizers. These writings presuppose the ability to decipher their veiled allusions to persons and events. Scholars have classified different types of prophecy, vision, and speech within such writings. One common sequence of themes in apocalyptic predictions has five elements: (1) evil times; (2) divine intervention; (3) divine judgment; (4) punishment of the wicked; and (5) deliverance and rejoicing of the righteous. Here is an example of a revelatory speech on salvation and judgment from 1 Enoch 1:3–9. Enoch is speaking:

Concerning the elect I said, and took up my parable about them: The Holy Great One will come forth from His dwelling, and the eternal God will tread upon earth, on Mount Sinai, [and appear from His camp] and appear in the strength of His might from the [highest] heaven. And all will be struck with fear, and the Watchers [referring to rebellious angels] will quake, and great fear and trembling will seize them to the ends of the earth. And the high mountains will be shaken,

and the high hills be made low, and melt like wax before the flame.
And the earth will be [completely] torn apart, and all that is upon the
earth will perish, and there will be a judgment on all. But with the
righteous He will make peace, and will protect the elect and mercy
will be upon them. And behold, He comes with ten thousands of his
holy ones (i.e., angels) to execute judgment on all, and to destroy the
wicked: and to convict all flesh of all the evil works which they have
committed, and of all the things which the wicked sinners have said
against Him.

In this vision God comes to Sinai as the divine warrior. God's
coming brings judgment and destruction to the wicked, mercy
and peace to the righteous.

Other oracles in the Enoch tradition detail the sins for which
the wicked will be punished. They bear false witness, oppress
others, and persecute the righteous:

Woe to you witnesses of falsehood! And to those who prepare oppression, for you shall soon perish. Woe to you sinners, for you persecute the
righteous! For you shall be handed over and be persecuted by oppression
and its yoke will lie heavy upon you. (1 En 95:6–7)

They have used violence and unjustice to gain great wealth.
Some may even think that the "wicked" are really righteous
persons:

Woe to you sinners! For your wealth makes you appear like the righteous, but your hearts reprimand you as sinners, this will be testimony
against you, as a record of your evil deeds. Woe to you who eat the best
bread and drink wine in large bowls, trampling upon the weak people
with your power. Woe to you who always have water available to you,
for you will soon be consumed and wither away, for you have fore-
saken the fountain of life. Woe to you who carry out oppression, deceit
and blasphemy! There will be a record of evil against you. Woe to you,
O powerful people! You who coerce the righteous with your power, the
day of your destruction is coming! In those days, at the time of your
condemnation, many and good days will come for the righteous ones.
(1 En 96:4–8)

The wicked lack wisdom; "they are devoid of knowledge and
wisdom, so they shall perish together with their goods and

with all their glory and honor" (1 En 98:3). They place a false confidence in the wealth they have piled up:

Woe to you who gain silver and gold by unjust means; you will then say, "We have grown rich and accumulated goods, we have acquired everything that we desired. So now let us do whatever we like; . . . "Your lies flow like water. For your wealth will not endure but it will take off from you quickly for you have acquired it all unjustly, and you shall be given over to a great curse. (1 En 97:8–10)

The condemnation of oppression and injustice in pursuit of wealth recalls the Old Testament prophets. However, the impending judgment is no longer limited to Israel's defeat by her enemies. It embraces the whole earth and all its inhabitants.

When the end time comes, God will intervene through heavenly agents. The pattern of sin, judgment, and restoration from Israel's salvation history is brought to a climax. The evils of the age in which the apocalyptic seer lives are the worst that have ever existed on earth. Mark 13:14–23 contains a collection of sayings about the woes of the last days. They will be so bad that even "the elect" would not survive if God had not shortened the days of tribulation (Mk 13:20). Mark 13:24–6 links judgment to the coming of the Son of man. The "Son of man" first appears as a heavenly figure whose ascent to God's throne signifies the salvation of the righteous in Daniel 7:13–14.

As the warnings against false prophets and messiahs in Mark 13:21–2 indicate, prophetic figures might claim to know the signs of the end time. They might lead people to follow them by claiming that they were inaugurating the last days. The prophecy in Malachi 4:5–6 (Hebrew text, 3:23–4) led to expectations that an Elijah figure would come to prepare the people before the coming of the Lord in judgment. In some cases Elijah's role is tied to that of Enoch (1 En 90:31; 4 Ezr 6:26). John the Baptist is the best-known preacher of repentance. He is identified with the Elijah figure in Matthew (11:13–14; 17:10–13).

We have less information about other figures who may have

claimed prophetic roles. Josephus speaks of "deceivers" who led the crowds into the desert with promises that they would repeat signs of God's deliverance (*Antiquities* xx.167–8; *War* ii.259). An Egyptian Jew led a crowd into the wilderness with promises to march on Jerusalem, seizing it through a divine intervention that would collapse the walls of the city (*Antiquities* xx.169–72; *War* ii.261–73; Acts 21:38). These examples suggest that some persons expected political deliverance for Israel through a miraculous reenactment of its exodus and conquest experiences.

Josephus also contains reports about individual prophets who were not leaders of movements. In 62 C.E. a certain Joshua ben Ananiah is said to have begun to prophesy against the Temple: "A voice from the east; a voice from the west; a voice from the four winds. A voice against Jerusalem and the temple, a voice against the bridegroom and the bride, a voice against all the people" (*War* vi.300–9). He continued to preach doom for seven years, despite attempts to silence him, and was at last killed during the Roman siege of Jerusalem in 70 C.E. However, Josephus does not indicate that Joshua ben Ananiah ever gained a following among the people.

We know very little about the social patterns of teaching and learning connected with apocalyptic visionaries and other prophetic figures. Those whom Josephus describes as leading the crowds to see signs and return to the founding experiences of Israel may not have transmitted any teaching to others. Their appeal lay in promises of new experiences of God's deliverance. Israel's enemies and their collaborators would be driven from the land. The nation could be reestablished on its ancient foundations.

Although John the Baptist preached repentance to the crowds, he also had a circle of disciples (cf. Mk 2:18; Lk 7:18; Jn 3:25). They continued to preach and baptize after their master's death (Acts 18:25; 19:3). But our only source for the Baptist's teaching are the few oracles preserved by Christians, who stressed John's role as forerunner to Jesus.

The apocalyptic writings show evidence of considerable editing and reinterpretation of earlier traditions. Activity of that sort suggests that there was some form of scribal teaching and learning associated with the written works designated as apocalyptic. The classic examples of apocalyptic writing within the New Testament, Mark 13 and Revelation, also draw on earlier written traditions to shape their prophecies. But John the Baptist and Jesus do not engage in this formal mode of interpretation and instruction. Their preaching uses apocalyptic themes to deliver a message to the crowd orally. The Baptist summons the people of Israel to repent because the time of God's judgment is approaching. Jesus announces that God's Rule is already present. People can enter the Kingdom if they recognize the opportunity to follow Jesus' vision of what it means to live according to the will of God. People will be judged on the basis of whether or not they have responded to Jesus' preaching of the Rule of God.

Clearly, only an upper-class minority had the wealth and leisure to pursue the kind of learning that went on in the more formal school settings of antiquity. Only they could travel to centers like Athens or Jerusalem to hear famous philosophers or teachers of the Law. Only they could pay teachers to come and instruct them, their families, and their associates. Only they could obtain the hand-copied scrolls on which the teachings of the philosophers, the Jewish Scriptures, the commentaries on the Law, the sayings of wise men, the apocalyptic prophecies of the seers, and the like were contained.

The rest of society learned the wise sayings when people used them in conversation or when they told stories about the deeds of wise people. They learned the opinions of philosophers from preachers like the Cynics who harangued the crowds in public places. Some basic stories or themes from philosophy might also find their way into the grammar school exercises. Jewish people learned about the Law from synagogue sermons and from popular preachers like John the Baptist. Local priests or scribes might tell them how to observe certain feasts or other provisions of the Law. Stories about their famous ancestors like Joseph also played a role in teaching the people. Prophetic figures like John the Baptist carried on the tradition of addressing new warnings and instructions from God to the people directly. As we turn to the picture of Jesus as teacher presented in the Gospels, we will find that his teaching shares both style and content with a number of the different forms of teaching that were in existence in his time.

Chapter 2

Jesus, Charismatic Teacher and Prophet

Established "schools" had a process by which persons became teachers. They would have to spend years as students or disciples of a famous teacher. An outstanding student would then succeed the master. Others might eventually form their own group. We have already seen that Jesus did not come out of such a school. He had not studied the Law with a famous scribe or been part of a group devoted to interpreting the Scriptures like the Pharisees or Essenes. This fact about Jesus lies behind the question preserved in John 7:15: "How does he know letters, since he has not been taught?" This comment does not imply that Jesus was illiterate. He would have been taught to read the Torah scrolls as well as the other forms of reading and writing common in elementary education. But it suggests that Jesus had not been taught how to interpret the Scriptures according to the principles of some school.

Jesus' reply was that he has been taught by God, the one who sent him. Anyone really concerned with doing God's will should recognize the source of his teaching and follow him (Jn 7:16–17). Another scene in John shows that early followers of Jesus also had to face the accusation from Jewish teachers that they were ignorant and could not presume to tell others the truth about God's will. This conflict is "acted out" in a story in which a blind man defends Jesus before hostile Jewish teachers. He is eventually thrown out of the synagogue for believing that Jesus is "from God" (Jn 9:13–34).

Scholars have picked up a word from sociology, "charismatic," to describe persons who become leaders outside the normal patterns by which societies grant some people authority to control the actions or beliefs of others. When we say that Jesus is a charismatic teacher, we are saying two things: first, that he does not have the normal status, authority, or power systems to back up what he says, and second, that he is able to convey his message to groups of people through his personal appeal. These characteristics might be used by a sociologist to describe many different types of leaders. Within the Bible there are additional overtones to the idea of "charism." The word itself refers to anointing. In the Hebrew Scriptures, special persons were designated by God's Spirit and often "anointed" to lead the people. God has chosen this particular individual and provides the power or inspiration needed for the task. The early leaders of the tribes of Israel who were called "judges" – kings like Saul and David – and even prophets could all be spoken of as charismatic leaders or teachers.

According to this view, "charismatic" does not refer to the personality of an individual and its impact on others. Rather, the word implies that the person has received a calling from God to undertake a particular mission. Such leaders and teachers represent God's own loving faithfulness and care for the people.

Jesus' Call and John the Baptist

The story of a person's divine call was often used to bolster the individual's claim to rule or speak for God. When the priest at God's sanctuary wanted to stop him from speaking, the eighth-century B.C.E. Hebrew prophet, Amos, pointed out that God had taken him from secular occupations to prophesy. He was not a member of a prophetic guild (Am 7:14–16). Paul referred to his "call" by the risen Lord in defense of his message that salvation could come to non-Jews on the basis of faith in Christ (Gal 1:11–16).

The synoptic Gospels narrate a "call" of Jesus in the scene of

Jesus' baptism (Mt 3:13–17; Mk 1:9–11; Lk 3:21–22). Each gospel has told the story differently. Matthew and Luke, who used Mark's gospel in their own writing, have reshaped the Marcan episode to fit the story line of their gospels. For their readers, the infancy narratives have already provided an introduction to who Jesus is and where he comes from. They have already shown that Jesus was chosen from conception to be God's spokesperson and the savior of the people. They must explain how Jesus came to be associated with the Baptist, since that link might otherwise suggest that Jesus was a disciple of John's. Luke's infancy narrative set the stage for the relationship by showing that John recognized Jesus' superiority even in the womb (Lk 1:39–45).

Matthew adds a dialogue between John and Jesus that shows that John acknowledges Jesus' superiority and that Jesus "approves" the Baptist's ministry as preparation for his own (3:14–15). At the same time, the reader is introduced to Jesus as the one who "fulfills all righteousness," a theme that is repeated in connection with Jesus' teaching in Matthew 5:17.

Both Luke and Matthew have changed the role of the heavenly voice. In Mark 1:10–11, Jesus' baptism leads to a vision in which he sees the open heavens and the Spirit, and hears God's voice addressed to him, since the "you" in the Greek is singular and not plural: "You are my beloved Son, with whom I am well pleased." Luke and Matthew depict these events as a sign to the assembled crowd. This scene identifies Jesus as the "Son" or servant of the Lord. The descent of the Spirit indicates that God will be acting through Jesus' ministry. Unlike the "call stories" of Old Testament prophets (Is 6:1–13; Jer 1:5–19; Ez 1–2), we are not told anything about Jesus' inner experience, about a particular commission given to him, or about his reply. These differences in form suggest that the baptism scene was not intended to present Jesus as a prophet like those familiar to the people from the Old Testament.

The reader is prepared for Jesus' coming by the gospel portraits of John the Baptist. John left his mark on history by being linked to the ministry of Jesus as "forerunner." John the Baptist functioned as a prophetic voice in his own right, however. The crowds may have expected Jesus to follow the type of preaching begun by the Baptist. The Jewish historian Josephus says that popular opinion attributed a military defeat suffered by Herod to God's anger with the king for executing John:

Some of the Jews thought that Herod's army had been destroyed by God and that he had been justly punished by God because of the execution of John, called the Baptist. For Herod put to death this good man who was exhorting the Jews to live upright lives, in dealing justly with one another and submitting to God, and to join in baptism. Indeed, it seemed to John that even this washing would not be acceptable as a pardon for sins, but only as a purification for the body, unless the soul had previously been cleansed through upright conduct. When still others joined the crowds around him, because they were quite enthusiastic in listening to his words, Herod became frightened that such persuasiveness with the people might lead to some uprising; for it seemed that they might go to any length on his advice. (*Antiquities* xviii.5)

In this passage, Josephus presents the Baptist as a moral reformer. Baptism purifies only the body; the rest of a person's life has to be changed by devotion to God and to treating others justly. The Gospels stress an additional feature of John's preaching, not mentioned in Josephus. His call to repent was based on the claim that God would soon judge the world (see Lk 3:7–9; Mt 3:11–12).

Like the Baptist, Jesus went about preaching to the crowds. He too spoke of God's Rule breaking into human history. Unlike the Baptist, Jesus did not become known for prescribing a water baptism to symbolize a person's renewed life of holiness. The earliest Christians, however, returned to the practice of baptism to express the new relationship between the believer and Jesus.

Jesus' Disciples Break with Their World

The story of John the Baptist has already introduced the idea of two ways in which a person might respond to preaching like that of the Baptist and Jesus. Most people would remain in their ordinary lives and relationships, but would seek to live with a new devotion to God. They might also treat others differently as a result. Luke 3:10–14 portrays the Baptist giving advice to three groups about how they should live:

1. "The crowds" should share what they have with those who have nothing (v. 11).
2. "Tax collectors" must avoid the greed and extortion for which the group as a whole was known and take care to collect only those taxes that were really owed (vv. 12–13).
3. "Soldiers" are also told to avoid certain characteristic vices of their class, robbing the subject population by violence or fraud, and grumbling over wages (v. 14).

Although Luke has put this teaching in the mouth of the Baptist, he certainly intended his Christian readers to recognize that it was addressed to them as well.

Most of those who accepted Jesus' preaching would have seen it as addressed to their daily lives. However, Jesus also gathered a group of disciples who made a much more radical break with everyday life. Luke presents the "paradigm" for this type of disciple in the calling of Peter (Lk 5:1–11). Jesus summons Peter, James, and John to leave their lives as fishermen and follow him. They will be involved in Jesus' ministry of preaching. Luke 8:1–3 reports that in addition to the "twelve," who accompanied Jesus on his preaching mission, several women who had been healed by Jesus were also part of the mission. They were apparently women who had inherited property that they were using to support Jesus and his disciples.

In our mobile society it is not too shocking to hear of people changing their life-style, even abandoning family and friends, and moving to some other part of the world. We all know of people who have done that in order to spread a message of peace and justice by contributing their lives and talent to development in a poor area of the world. Even if they are not engaged in converting others to the religious message of Christianity, many of these people have been inspired by Christian ideals and will work under the sponsorship or protection of organizations that have their roots in Christianity. Of course we may be surprised if one of our children, students, friends, or associates does something like this, but we can understand what they are doing and why.

In Jesus' time such forms of "uprooting" were evidence that disasters like war and famine had destroyed the traditional society of villages and towns. In that society children followed the occupations of their parents unless displaced by natural disaster, war, or enslavement. People lived in the same communities for generations. Priests, scribes, and Levites would be the sons of other priests, scribes, and Levites. They would also marry the daughters of such persons. Peter, James, and John were fishermen because their fathers were fishermen, and so on.

The traditional villager would have been quite shocked to have Jesus and his followers break with the ancestral ways of life. The Gospels report that even Jesus' relatives were concerned. They were not sure what had happened to him. Jesus' enemies argued that anyone who behaved as he did must be "crazy" (i.e., possessed by Satan; see Mk 3:20–35). Jesus defends himself by insisting that his preaching and healing are a sign that God's Rule is destroying the power of Satan. He then insists that the true test of "family" is not blood relationships but doing the will of God.

It is important to remember this social context of Jesus' summons to discipleship when we read some of the radical sayings in the Gospels about abandoning home and family ties. In Jesus' culture, people who broke with their families and "home territory" might experience that as losing their identity. Practically everything about a person was determined by the place and patterns of relationship into which he or she was born. The life cycle did not include a period of adolescence in which people spent time asking what they would do as a trade or whom they would marry or where they would live. A person's family would settle things like that just as families do in some traditional cultures today. Read the Parable of the Prodigal Son from this perspective (Lk 15:11–32), and note how quickly the younger son loses his identity and moral character when he leaves his father's farm.

Naturally those young men who left home to study with a famous teacher in Jerusalem or to join a religious sect like the Essenes had a substitute for the parental identity they left. But Jesus was not established as a teacher like the famous rabbis of later generations. Mark 6:1–6 reports that people in Jesus' own hometown were the most skeptical about him. That skepticism is the negative side of a traditional society. A person's identity is thought to be fixed. Someone like Jesus who breaks the established patterns of life would have a very difficult time persuading others that he is right to do so. And it certainly must have been difficult for the disciples to accept Jesus' call to break with their own families and occupations to follow him.

The Gospels preserve a number of radical sayings that show that a disciple must be ready to give up all these relationships for Jesus. Jesus does not claim that having a family, home, or occupation cuts a person off from God. But he insists that it would be wrong if a person who had a calling to serve God in some particular way let family or anxieties about material things cancel out that call. Jesus warns a would-be follower that he himself has become even more homeless than the animals (Mt 8:18–20). An even more shocking saying says that following Jesus must take priority over funeral rites for one's father (Mt 8:21–22). Jesus tells his disciples that they are not to concern themselves with making sure they have the material goods necessary for their mission. They will have to rely on the goodwill and hospitality of the people to whom they preach (Mt 10:9–11).

How does Jesus deal with the anxiety that such a way of life creates? He insists that just as God cares for all things in creation, so God hears and cares for those who are doing God's work (Mt 6:25–33; 10:29–31). He points out that people who do nothing but worry about making themselves "secure" have no control over much of their lives. Thieves can always steal your money (Mt 6:19). A rich person can drop dead right in the middle of plans to expand and make even more money (Lk 12:16–21). Trusting that God will provide for those who have committed themselves to the Kingdom is not so foolish as we may feel. Of course, as we have seen, Jesus does not assume that God is going to work miracles in order to care for his followers. Jesus points to the hospitality and goodness of other people who will aid the disciples. Luke 12:33 speaks of those who will sell possessions and give to the poor as their way of entering the Kingdom.

Jesus' Message Is for All

Many teachers had a limited audience. They spoke to educated persons, most often men, who were seeking some higher insight into interpreting the Law or "wisdom" about divine things or the teaching of a philosophical school. The "prophetic" character of John the Baptist and Jesus is shown in the fact that they are not primarily teachers of specialized disciples. They both appealed to the crowds. God was calling the whole nation in repentance. The authorities were alarmed by the influence both men had over the crowds. Such fears apparently led to the deaths of both John the Baptist and Jesus.

Their preaching drew on the Old Testament tradition in

which the prophetic call to repentance and renewal before God's judgment is addressed to Israel. Those who obeyed and repented would make up the "remnant" or the true Israel, which would be vindicated at the judgment. A prophetic word attributed to the Baptist (Mt 3:7–10; Lk 3:7–9) warns against relying on descent from Abraham for salvation. God can raise up new "children" for Abraham even from the stones. Divine judgment is imminent. People must show the fruits of holiness in their lives.

The Gospels suggest that Jesus did more than call a sinful people to renewed righteousness as the prophets had done before him. They preserve slanders against Jesus for associating with "tax collectors and sinners" (e.g., Lk 5:30; 7:34; Mt 11:19; 15:1–2). This expression is intended to cover all persons who were outcasts in Palestinian society. The expression "sinner" could refer to two groups: (1) Jews who had abandoned the obligations of the Mosaic Law but could be reconciled to God if they repented; or (2) non-Jews, who were considered "sinners" by definition, since they were without the Law and did not worship God. "Tax collectors" are associated with other groups of sinners in the Gospels: "robbers, evildoers, adulterers" (Lk 18:11); "harlots" (Mt 21:32); and "non-Jews" (Mt 18:17). Dishonesty and extortion were commonly associated with persons who collected taxes and tariffs (e.g., Lk 3:12–13).

Luke 7:33–4 (Mt 11:18–19) contrasts the Baptist's ascetic life, his abstaining from food, with Jesus' enjoyment of meals in quite diverse company. People called the Baptist "possessed" (Lk 7:33) and Jesus a "glutton and drunkard, friend of tax collectors and sinners" (Lk 7:34). The Baptist's behavior points up the repentance called for in his preaching. However, many people did not see it as a "sign" for their times; they dismissed John as "demon possessed" or, as we might say today, a "crackpot" or "fanatic." Jesus comes living the life of an ordinary person and is dismissed as wanton. Since this is directed at Jesus by those who reject his teaching and is parallel in calling the Baptist possessed, it cannot be taken as evidence that Jesus does not adopt a way of life that set him apart from other Jews. He does not follow special rules about food, drink, and clothing that mark him as a holy person.

The saying appended in Luke 7:35 affirms that both the Baptist and Jesus are "Wisdom's children." They are the messengers sent by divine wisdom (see Wis 7:27) and rejected by a foolish generation. Luke concludes the previous section with a comment modeled on this proverbial saying. Luke 7:29–30 speaks of "all the people, even toll-collectors" accepting John's baptism and thus "vindicating God," while the Pharisees and those learned in the Law reject John and "God's plan."

Luke's division between those (including outcasts like toll collectors) who accept God's plan of salvation and teachers of the Law who reject it seems to oversimplify the situation. Luke 13:31, for example, preserves an early piece of tradition in which Pharisees warn Jesus about a plot against him. Luke 5:17 included them among those who came to hear Jesus. Matthew preserves the traditions of Jewish Christians who found in Jesus' teaching the true interpretation of the Law (e.g., Mt 5:17–20). Such evidence suggests that Jesus' appeal to the crowds was not based simply on his rejection of what people had learned in the Law as the way to holiness.

The Gospels often differentiate between the "crowds" and the "disciples." The latter receive teaching from Jesus in private (e.g., Mk 4:10–20; 7:17–23; 10:10–11, 23–31) as well as witnessing his public teaching. Christian readers will identify with the disciples. Jesus' teachings on mission (Mt 10:16–42) reflect both the hostility and the unexpected kindness to which the first Christians were subject. The picture of Jesus surrounded by disciples makes it evident that he is understood as a teacher and not simply a wandering miracle-worker.

However, the crowd–disciples contrast also creates some difficulties in understanding the audience of Jesus' teaching. Matthew 10:1–4 prefaces the mission discourse with the list of the twelve. Mark 6:7 (also Lk) mentions only that the twelve were sent. Does this division mean that a different level of teaching or holiness was required of the disciples chosen to spread Jesus' message about the Reign of God? Most scholars think that Jesus did not intend to create a special class of disciples with its own rules of holiness. Nor was the spread of the gospel limited to the twelve.

Luke 10:1 meets this problem by speaking of an additional group sent out on mission. Their instructions are based on material associated with the sending of the twelve, a tradition preserved in Luke 9:1–6. The episode in Luke 10 appears to be a parallel tradition used by Luke to show that others will be associated with the mission. Luke 10:2 links the additional "sending" with a saying about the abundant harvest (cf. Mt 9:37–8; Jn 4:36–8). "Harvest" is used as an image for God's judgment in the Hebrew Scriptures (cf. Jl 4:1–13; Is 27:11–12). Luke reflects this imagery by adding the woes against towns in which Jesus had preached to this mission charge (10:13–15). As persons "sent" by Jesus, those who preach the gospel represent Jesus and ultimately God. Accepting or rejecting their preaching is equivalent to accepting or rejecting Jesus (Lk 10:16).

Luke has used this episode to show the reader that participation in Jesus' ministry was not limited to the twelve. Jesus is able to select an additional seventy(-two) from among his followers. A larger group of witnesses to Jesus' ministry is presumed by the selection of Matthias in Acts 1:23–6. If we understand Jesus' teaching as directed primarily to the "crowds" and as creating a larger group of followers than the twelve, an additional question remains: Were women disciples of Jesus?

Again Luke provides some of the most explicit hints that they were. Luke 8:1–3 includes several prominent women along with the twelve in Jesus' Galilean ministry. The association of women with a male teacher seems to have been a striking departure from cultural norms. John 4:27 has Jesus' disciples comment disparagingly on his conversation with the Samaritan woman, who served the Johannine community as a model for a woman believer and missionary (Jn 4:7–42). Although Mary Magdalene is well known in early Christian tradition, Joanna, identified as wife of the manager of one of Herod's estates, and Susanna are otherwise unknown. Luke may depend on an early tradition for the list of names. These women are able to use their own possessions to provide for Jesus and his followers.

Luke 8:19–21 recasts the Marcan tradition about disbelief among Jesus' relatives (cf. Mk 3:20–1, 31–3) to include Jesus' mother and brothers among those who hear the word of God (also see Lk 1:38; 2:19, 51). Jesus' women followers are present at the cross (23:49), discover the empty tomb (24:10), and are included with the twelve and Jesus' relatives in the group awaiting the Spirit in Jerusalem (Acts 1:14).

The picture of women disciples should not be limited to the "service" they provide for Jesus and the others. As "hearers of God's Word," they too receive the teaching of Jesus. The story of Martha and Mary in Luke 10:38–42 makes this point clear. It repeats the lesson of Luke 8:21: Listening to the word takes priority over all other concerns. The picture of Mary at Jesus' feet makes it clear that she is receiving instruction just as male disciples would have done. Martha's preoccupation with preparing Jesus' meal has kept her from the role of student (v. 40). When Jesus asserts that Mary "has chosen the good part" (Lk 10:42), he breaks with society's expectation that women should behave as Martha does and busy themselves honoring Jesus with a special meal. Jesus insists that he does not require "hospitality" (cf. rejection of preoccupation with physical needs, Lk 8:18; 21:34). Martha should drop her preparations and join her sister (Lk 10:42a, "one thing is necessary").

The Johannine tradition preserved another story about Martha and Mary that shows them to have been friends of Jesus.

There Martha learns that Jesus is "resurrection and life" (Jn 11:1–44).

These stories in which women are remembered as disciples of Jesus, not simply members of the larger crowd that came to hear him, raise questions about passages in the Gospels that seem to exclude them from any public role as disciples. This pattern is evident in Mark. Women are acknowledged to have been "followers" of Jesus (Mk 15:40; 16:8), but in the gospel narrative they are never part of the "inner circle" of those around Jesus. It is this "inner circle" that receives private teaching from Jesus (Mk 4:11, 33–4). Women are "hidden" in the crowd scenes, which refer to "men" apart from women and children (Mk 6:44; 14:21) or mention them in passing (9:35–7; 10:13–16). With the exception of the woman with the hemorrhage, who approached Jesus in the midst of a crowd (5:24–34), women are always healed at home, not in public. The Syro-Phoenecian woman who wins healing for her daughter in debate with Jesus is a Gentile and thus an outsider (7:24–30).

The episode about children being brought to Jesus (Mk 10:13–16) at one stage in the tradition may have been similar to the Martha and Mary story. Marriage contracts from this period sometimes included stipulations on how far a wife might go from her home without her husband's permission. She had to be able to return within the day. She could check on wandering children and livestock and visit neighbors and relatives who lived nearby. The "they" bringing children to Jesus would be village women of this sort. Bringing their children also enabled them to hear Jesus' word. By rejecting attempts to keep the children away, Jesus affirms the place of women among his followers. If the children were pushed aside, then the women looking after them would have to return to their homes. By accepting the children, Jesus enables their mothers to hear his word and become believers.

However, the passage as we have it in Mark has been shifted away from its emphasis on inclusiveness among Jesus' disciples by the addition of the sayings on "becoming like a child" to enter the Reign of God (vv. 14b–15). The saying appears independently in Matthew 18:3 and in a variant tradition in the second-century collection of Jesus' sayings transmitted by the Gnostics, the Gospel of Thomas (Saying 22). It may also underlie the dialogue in John 3:3–5 on rebirth through the Spirit. Other sayings of Jesus use the child to exemplify the attitude toward "greatness" that Jesus' followers should have. They allude to receiving a child as equivalent to receiving Jesus (Mk 9:33–7; Mt 18:1–6; Lk 9:46–8).

Another episode in which the actions of women in Jesus' entourage are a source of conflict among the men surrounding Jesus is Jesus' anointing by a woman (Mk 14:3–9; Mt 26:6–13; also Jn 12:1–8 and Lk 7:36–50). The Johannine version of the story identifies the woman as Martha's sister Mary and the protesting disciple as Judas. But the basic structure of the story follows that in Mark and Matthew. The woman who anoints Jesus recognizes what his male disciples do not: that he is the suffering servant about to die. Her insight into Jesus' true identity and the divine plan of salvation is vindicated by Jesus. In that situation the pious reasoning of the disciples is rejected just like that of the scribes and Pharisees who had been outraged by Jesus' attitude toward the Sabbath.

Luke's version of this story is quite different. Jesus' anointing has been conflated with the Parable of the Two Debtors (7:41–3) and a story of the pardoning of a sinful woman. Jesus' opponent is Simon, a Pharisee who protests the fact that Jesus, renowned as a prophet, does not stop the sinner from touching him. Jesus defends the woman's gesture as an act of hospitality and love that forms a sharp contrast to the deficiencies of Simon's hospitality. The story shows Luke's reader that forgiveness and salvation have come to one of the despised of Israel. The woman has shown the superiority of her love and faith to that of Jesus' host. This point is underlined by the

Parable of the Two Debtors (Lk 7:40–2), since even Simon recognizes that the debtor who had been forgiven a larger sum would love the creditor more (v. 43). The sinful woman, scorned by righteous people, is more open to God's love and mercy than the Pharisee Simon. Thus this story defends the association with "tax collectors and sinners" for which Jesus was criticized.

The gospel narratives present us with a tension between inherited traditions about the openness of Jesus' teaching to all persons, sinners, the outcast, even women and children, and the narrower group of disciples identified as the twelve. The Marcan picture of Jesus as a public teacher surrounded by male disciple-students has been seen by some scholars as an accommodation to Hellenistic stereotypes of the philosopher-teacher. Women who learned from philosopher-teachers did so in the home, where a teacher might give private instruction to friends of the patron or patroness. The few Hellenistic women known for philosophical wisdom usually followed the footsteps of male relatives, either fathers or brothers.

The traditions that represent Jesus as teacher interacting with women challenge this stereotype. Jesus commends "hearing the word" to women disciples. He defends their insight and deeds as true to the salvation God intends. He makes it possible for women to approach him by accepting the children they bring with them.

Jesus' teaching is not addressed to an elite. One does not have to have the opportunity for special education and training as students in philosophical schools did. One does not have to belong to a group like the Essenes or Pharisees, who had shaped all aspects of life around understanding the righteousness in the Law. The Syro-Phoenecian woman and the Samaritan woman show that a person did not even have to be Jewish to understand Jesus' message about the Reign of God and to share in its benefits.

Chapter 3

The Style of Jesus' Teaching

Jesus spoke with a prophetic voice to all people. Understanding his message did not require special education or even a life that had been marked by holiness in a special way. Ordinary people heard Jesus' words as the word of God addressed to them. Jesus did not use a "scholarly" or "technical language" such as we find in philosophical writings of the time or in legal disputes over the meaning of the Law. The references to the Law and other images taken from the Hebrew Scriptures are ones that would have been well known to Jesus' audience. Other images in Jesus' teaching reflected the daily life and experience of people.

Since we do not live in Jesus' world as part of our "everyday life," we often have to use the findings of archaeology and the study of other writings from the time to understand Jesus' images. Even then we may not be sure whether Jesus is simply reporting what people did or whether he has exaggerated a commonplace situation in order to make a point. The well-known Parable of the Sower (Mk 4:3–8) is a good example of this problem:

A sower went out to sow. And as he sowed, some seed fell along the path, and the birds came and devoured it. Other seed fell on rocky ground, where it had not much soil, and immediately it sprang up, since it had no depth of soil; and when the sun rose it was scorched, and since it had no root it withered away. Other seed fell among thorns and the thorns grew up and choked it, and it yielded no grain. And other seeds fell into good soil and brought forth grain, growing up and increasing and yielding thirtyfold and sixtyfold and a hundredfold.

Most of us plow up our gardens and prepare the soil before sowing seed. We do not toss seed on rocky ground. Roman treatises on agriculture show that plowing before sowing was also the usual practice in the first-century Mediterranean.

Other scholars have found references in rabbinic writings and the following story from Jubilees 11:10–13 to suggest that seed was scattered first and then plowed in:

And prince Mastema sent crows and birds so that they might eat the seed which was being sown in the earth in order to spoil the earth so that they might rob humans of their labors. Before they plowed in the seed, crows picked it off the surface of the earth. . . . And the years began being barren because of the crows. . . . If ever they were able to save a little from all of the fruit of the earth in their days, it was with great effort.

The author of Jubilees goes on to explain that the fourteen-year-old Abraham saves the people from the crows by sending the birds back to the heavens before they land. The people were able to harvest enough food to eat. Then Abraham changes the design of plows so that the farmers are able to feed the seed down along the plow handle as they plow. Thus the seed is buried immediately and the crows are not able to get to it (Jubilees 11:18–24). Scholars date Jubilees to the second century B.C.E. The story about Abraham turns on an agricultural innovation that changed the practice of sowing and plowing.

What about the sower in Jesus' parable? Our evidence leaves a number of possibilities open. Perhaps, Jesus was simply describing the way in which crops were sown. The story draws a lesson from the facts of everyday life in Galilean villages. Or, the sower was acting in a way that appeared foolish or outdated. In that case, the hearer would conclude that it is a miracle that he got such a harvest. Another possibility is that Jesus and his audience were familiar with the Abraham legend. In that case, Jesus would be suggesting that the harvest in his story comes without miraculous intervention or the latest agricultural technology. A final possibility is that Jesus was not thinking about agricultural practice at all but about passages in which the Hebrew Scripture speaks of how the word of God or the wisdom of God comes to humans. Those who receive and attend to it gain a rich harvest (e.g., Is 55:10–11; Ecclus 6:18–21). The allusions to Scripture can be combined with any of the first three possibilities. Since other parables also seem to combine an echo of Scripture with an image from everyday experience, we may assume that such is the case here as well. We cannot decide with certainty what Jesus' audience assumed to be the normal routine of plowing and sowing. Archaeology might someday provide evidence that would clarify the issue.

Although the general image of a sower losing seed to various natural causes but reaping a large harvest remains the same, our decision about the question of plowing changes our perception of the impact of the story. A combination of (1) the view that the sower acts as any villager would have and (2) allusions from Scripture to sowing God's word would leave the audience agreeing that Jesus has made a point from experience and Scripture that is typical of other wisdom teachers.

Combinations of the view that the sower was acting foolishly or an allusion to the Abraham legend found in Jubilees and the Scripture references create different levels of tension in the audience. Assuming that the sower was acting contrary to usual practice might lead people to think, What a fool! He doesn't even know how to run a farm. Assuming a reference to the Abraham story might lead in a slightly different direction, since Jesus would be talking about a sower living in the legendary time before the wisdom of Abraham improved agricultural technology. In both cases the apparent success of the harvest stands in tension with the hearer's initial reaction to the setting.

Questions like these result from the distance between our world and that of Jesus. Opinion is equally divided over whether the amount of the harvest represents an unusually large yield or is simply a way of speaking about a "good harvest." Again scholars can produce evidence on both sides.

Scholarly attempts to collect the evidence needed to understand the images in Jesus' parables often make it seem that his teaching is very complicated. But we need to remember that Jesus' audience could relate to these images directly just as we do to a reference to some event in the history of our country, to some common piece of writing like a popular song or advertisement or best-selling book, to a popular film, to a joke or a political cartoon. Sometimes we find that we have to stop and explain to friends from other countries or to children or others who do not share the same experiences. That fact reminds us that even in Jesus' audience there may have been different responses depending on the background of particular individuals. That is why even if we could answer all of our questions about Jesus' time, we would still be left with the possibility of different understandings of Jesus' words. The Parable of the Sower presents an image of that situation. Sowing the same seed does not always produce the same results.

The image of the sower is not simply taken from daily practice or legend, however. Jesus could also have been reminding his audience of Scripture references in which the harvest or lack of it refers to the word of God or to human wisdom and folly. Isaiah 55:10–11 occurs in a prophetic text that assures the reader that God's word is not empty. No matter what the doubters may say, the Lord's promises of salvation will be accomplished if the people persevere in justice and righteousness. God does not reject the people. Sirach 6:18–21 is a piece of proverbial wisdom directed at the young. Those who cultivate wisdom will reap a rich harvest.

The preaching of the Baptist (e.g., Mt 3:10, 12) introduces another use of harvest imagery. It appears in apocalyptic prophecies for the end-time judgment of God. This use of the image is based on prophetic texts that spoke of God's judgment of a sinful people in harvest images (e.g., Is 21:10; Mi 4:12; Jl 3:13). This parable, then, points to four aspects of Jesus' teaching that we will explore in this chapter: proverb, parable, prophetic word, and apocalyptic image. In addition, we will also look at sayings of Jesus that refer to the interpretation of the Law of Moses.

Proverbs and Parables: Jesus and the Wisdom Tradition

We have seen that Jesus' teaching can be linked to the wisdom traditions of Israel. He often uses short sayings that communicate familiar truths or observations about human experience. We usually call such sayings "proverbs." Scholars have found a number of different types of proverbs in the Bible: based on direct correspondence or association, on contrast, on what is futile or absurd, on the characteristics of persons like the foolish or the lazy, on proper priorities, or on the consequences of actions. Sometimes the word "proverb" is used to refer to more general types of figurative speech like a parable (Jn 10:6) or a longer wisdom discourse (Jb 13:12). When proverbs are collected as they are in the Book of Proverbs, they present general instructions about how to live one's life.

Frequently, proverbial sayings of Jesus occur in short stories (referred to as "apothegms" or "pronouncement stories" in scholarly literature) that supply a context for understanding how a saying is being applied. The sayings about the new and old wineskins or the patched garment are good examples of the way in which the story setting interprets the proverb (Mk 2:21–2; Mt 9:16–17; Lk 5:36b–8). By themselves these sayings could be used for any situation in which a person tried to do something foolish that mixes old and new materials resulting in the loss of both. But in the Gospels the sayings are part of an extended defense of Jesus' disciples. They do not fast like the disciples of the Baptist or the Pharisees.

Another familiar proverb that begins with the expression "No one . . . " refers to a lamp on a lampstand (Mk 4:21; Mt 5:15; Lk 8:16; 11:33). Matthew has used the saying as an exhortation to disciples to show their belief to others. Mark 4:21 (and Lk 8:16 following Mk) attaches this saying to the exposition of the Parable of the Sower. The verses that follow (Mk 4:22–5) exhort the reader to hear the message of the parables. A call to hear the word and obey it is introduced by the saying in Luke 11:33. There, the saying is "allegorized" by appeal to another saying about the eye and the body. (This wisdom saying appears separately in Mt 6:22–3.) Light refers allegorically to a person's understanding of the message being preached by Jesus.

These examples show that even within the Gospels the proverbial sayings of Jesus are not "pinned down" to a single application. The same saying may appear in different forms. It may be used to make more than one point. A context for interpreting a saying may be given in the story of a challenge to Jesus that the saying resolves. Or the context may be created by incorporating the saying into a series of sayings or a short "discourse."

A discourse made up of short sayings may be used by the author of a Gospel to comment on something that has happened in the narrative. This usage is evident in Luke 11:33–6:

No one after lighting a lamp puts it in a cellar or under a bushel, but on a stand that those who enter may see the light. Your eye is the lamp of your body; when your eye is sound, your body is full of light; but when it is not sound, your body is full of darkness. If then your whole body is full of light, having no part dark, it will be wholly bright, as when a lamp with its rays gives you light.

A proverb about the lamp on the stand is followed by another about the eye. The final sentence links the two independent sayings by making the first an illustration of the state of the body when the eye is "sound" or "whole." Thus, we have a short discourse created out of proverbial sayings.

Further inspection shows that Luke has created this discourse out of Jesus' sayings in order to comment on the previous episode. Physically, an "evil" or "unsound" eye means one in which the function of vision is impaired. Applications of the proverb will, of course, apply that image to any acts that stem from a person's evil character. The preceding episode condemns Jesus' generation for demanding signs (Lk 11:29–32). It begins with the statement "This generation is evil." The word "evil" leads the reader to associate those demanding the sign with persons who have an "evil eye." In commenting on his generation, Jesus contrasted them unfavorably with earlier generations, like the Ninevites, who repented when Jonah preached (v. 30). The sayings about the lamp and the eye now become a warning to the reader not to be part of the "evil generation."

What makes Jesus' use of proverbial traditions distinctive? Jesus is not simply teaching people truths of folk wisdom that they already have heard from others. As this comment on the lack of faith that Jesus finds in his own time shows, Jesus uses proverbs in defense of his vision of the Reign of God. Jesus wants people to see that it is time for a new experience of God's presence in human life. This new vision challenges old ways of thinking and acting. In order to show people how radical the challenge is, he often uses images that are extreme or even paradoxical. Unlike the commonplaces of much wisdom tradition, which say that the world will always go on as a place in which the fools repeat the same mistakes, Jesus sees the coming of the Reign of God as an opportunity for radical change.

Examples of such paradoxes include, "Everyone who exalts himself will be humbled, and one who humbles himself will be exalted" (Lk 14:11). When we compare that proverb with the common saying "Pride goeth before a fall," we can see the difference. We might use the latter of a champion athlete who has become arrogant from always winning but who is finally dethroned by a younger player. Or we might use it of someone who has become arrogant because of his or her business success but finally suffers a reversal. Jesus' proverb intensifies that common attitude by making it a general rule. The rule is backed up by the claim that God sees to the humbling of those who become arrogant or proud, since pride means setting oneself (not God) first. This idea is spelled out in the Magnificat (Lk 1:46–55):

He has shown strength with his arm, he has scattered the proud in the imagination of their hearts, he has put down the mighty from their thrones, and exalted those of low degree. He has filled the hungry with good things, and the rich he has sent away empty. (vv. 51–3).

Sometimes Jesus' sayings that suggest God will put down the rich and powerful and raise up the poor seem too extreme. Even Jesus' disciples are said to have protested when he commented, "It is easier for a camel to pass through the eye of a needle than for a rich person to enter the Kingdom of God" (Mk 10:25). Does God really exclude the rich and powerful from salvation? Does wealth separate persons from God? Or does the problem lie in the way in which many people obtain their wealth? In Judea and Galilee, the rich supported the Herods and the Romans who held the people captive. They may have gained land through property seized from others or taken for debts the farmers could not pay when the harvest was bad. They may have been toll collectors who charged more than they should. It would seem very difficult for a person who became rich in such ways to be righteous, just, and merciful toward others.

Even the Book of Proverbs thinks it is unlikely that a merchant could be a just person. Ecclesiasticus 26:20–27:2 says:

A merchant can hardly keep from wrongdoing, and a tradesman will not be declared innocent of sin. Many have committed sin for a trifle, and whoever seeks to get rich will avert his eyes. A stake is driven firmly into a crack between two stones, so sin is wedged in between buying and selling.

This image provides a sharp warning against being complacent about justice. The metaphor of a stake wedged between two stones is not quite as paradoxical as Jesus' image of a camel trying to get through the eye of a needle. When his disciples protested that no one would be able to be saved, Jesus answered that it might seem impossible for the rich to be saved, but God could still make their salvation possible.

Some of Jesus' sayings are extended sentences that could easily be expanded into short stories about the situations mentioned. They show the decisive response that a person who finds the Reign of God will make. Jesus even uses a merchant as an example of the kind of action a person should take in order to reach the Reign of God (Mt 13:45–6).

Another illustration Jesus gives is that of a day laborer working a field. He finds a treasure buried there, sells everything he has, and buys the field (Mt 13:44). Jesus' audience must have been surprised by that example. People often "lost" jewels and coins that had been buried or hidden in foundations of their houses for safekeeping. Both laws and legal suits show the original owners trying to recover such property from workers who had taken it from a wall or found it in family land that they had sold. But Jesus focuses our attention on the joy the finder experiences and his willingness to give everything to get possession of the treasure.

Parables Challenge the Imagination

These images used for the Reign of God show us that Jesus is not a cynical pessimist. No matter what human weakness, blindness, and folly seem to suggest, people can be converted. They can experience the joy of the Reign of God. Another way in which Jesus instills confidence that God's Reign can bring abundant goodness into the world is to use images from nature.

These images assure the hearer that even if it has very small beginnings, the Reign of God will bring a rich harvest.

Mark 4:26–9 speaks of the Kingdom resembling the mysterious growth of a seed. The expression "of itself" may be a reference to the sabbatical year when the land was supposed to be allowed to lie fallow. People could harvest only what grew on that land "of itself." This parable is followed by a comparison between the Kingdom and the small mustard seed. When the seed has produced a mustard bush it is a big enough shrub to shelter the birds (Mk 4:30–2). Even though the seed on the fallow land and the mustard bush might not seem very important, they both provide for the needs of those who depend on them.

Some of Jesus' more famous parables are short stories that often have a central figure who initiates a situation that demands a response, such as a master giving tasks to servants. The drama of the parable turns on the outcome. Frequently, one course of action leads to condemnation, another to salvation. Sometimes the successful character in the story surprises us. Here are some examples:

1. *The Good Samaritan* (Lk 10:30–7). The crisis has been created when a Jewish pilgrim has been beaten, robbed, and left for dead. Neither a priest nor a Levite (perhaps not wishing to incur the ritual impurity that would come from contact with a corpse) stops to help the man. A Samaritan not only helps but also pays for the victim to be cared for in an inn. In order to understand this story, we need to know that the Samaritans were descendants of Jews left when the Assyrians overran the northern kingdom in the eighth century B.C.E. They had their own version of the Mosaic Torah and refused to submit to the descendants of the southern kingdom centered in Jerusalem. There was bitter enmity between Jews and Samaritans. Jewish pilgrims traveling through Samaria to Jerusalem from Galilee were sometimes attacked by robbers from the Samaritan vil-

lages. We even know of cases in which bloody retaliation followed such an episode. It would have been as hard to imagine a Samaritan as the "loving neighbor" and "savior" of a Jew as it would be for us to imagine a Palestinian guerrilla appearing as a model of piety in the preaching of a Jewish teacher in Palestine today.

2. *The Unforgiving Servant* (Mt 18:23–34). Crises are created by the situations of two debtors. One servant owes a huge debt to a powerful king. The amount of the debt suggests that he was responsible for collecting revenues owed to the king and had failed to collect the amount required of him. His plea for time to repay is not very credible. The second servant owes the first a small personal debt that might indeed be repaid. Yet, much to the audience's surprise, the oriental potentate responds by forgiving the whole amount that the first servant owed! But when the second servant asks the first to give him more time to repay the small loan, the first does not even recognize his own plea in the words of the second servant, rejects the request, and seeks to have the debtor thrown into jail. His failure to respond with compassion leads to his downfall when other servants report back to the king, and the king revokes the forgiveness that he had extended to the man.

3. *The Servants Entrusted with the Master's Money* (Lk 19:12–26; Mt 25:14–30). Action is determined by the master entrusting his wealth to different servants when he must depart on a journey. All three servants know that a servant entrusted with the master's property is expected to increase the master's wealth. The first two are successful and are rewarded accordingly. The third uses the master's harsh character as an excuse for merely preserving the sum intact and consequently suffers the punishment for failing at his task that he apparently sought to avoid by not risking the master's money in order to make more.

Other parables of Jesus focus on a surprising, shocking or

unusual action by a central character. They too challenge Jesus' audience to reflect on their own behavior and actions. Very often, parables of this type have been used by the Gospel writers as reference points for particular moral lessons the Christian audience ought to learn. Sayings of Jesus may be added to the parable to make the application clear. Some examples of this type include:

1. *The Prodigal Son* (Lk 15:11–32). This parable is not the folk story, like the story of Joseph in the Hebrew Scriptures, of a younger son who goes far from home and returns triumphant. The younger son in Jesus' story demands that his father give him his inheritance and then wastes it in a foreign city in sexual immorality. A Jewish audience would have recognized that a foreign city had to be a gentile city in which the young man would be in danger of falling into the sexual and religious immorality that Jews associated with the Gentiles. When he is broke, the youth violates another Jewish rule by agreeing to serve as a swineherd, an occupation rejected by Jews, who do not eat pork and consider the pig unclean. When the owner does not give the boy anything to eat, he finally decides to return home, confess his wrongdoing, and even accept the status as servant rather than son. The father greets the return of his wayward son without any of the expected and well-deserved rebuke. On his return, his father treats him to a great celebration! The faithful elder brother, who will inherit the farm, protests such a welcome. Why should the bad son be given a huge celebration, when his own constant service had never merited even a small party for his friends? When he answers his elder son, the father affirms his relationship to the elder but insists that it is right to celebrate the return of the lost son. Jesus' audience must decide whether the elder's protest or the father's defense is to carry the day.

2. *The Great Banquet* (Lk 14:14–24; Mt 22:1–10). A wealthy man (a king in Matthew's version) gives a banquet (not an

everyday occurrence) and all the invited guests offer excuses for
not coming. While that may be every modern party giver's
nightmare, in ancient times it would have been an even more
astonishing breach of hospitality. Persons who were "clients"
(that is, in some way dependent on a wealthy person for ad-
vancement, business, or other favors) were obligated to respond
to such a summons. Even a person's equals would hardly take
lightly an invitation to a banquet.

What does the man do? Partly out of anger at the slight, he
does something no one would have thought of doing: He in-
vites the poor, homeless, anonymous persons from the area.
Matthew uses the parable as an allegory to warn Christians
against neglecting to follow the way of life laid out in Jesus'
teaching (see 7:13–28). Matthew wants to make sure that
Christians do not take salvation for granted because they have
been included in God's banquet. Verses 11–14 take what may
have been part of another parable as a more specific warning.
One must have proper dress and works of discipleship, or be
excluded from the Kingdom. Such an expansion cannot have
been part of the original parable, since it would be absurd to
think that the poor from the streets would have dress clothes.

3. *The Vineyard Owner and the Laborers* (Mt 20:1–13). During harvest season, owners had to hire day laborers to work
much as they do today. Usually such workers were in demand
during the harvest and could command a solid day's wage such
as the man offers the initial group. Like the father in the Parable of the Prodigal Son, the owner does something that appears
"unfair" to the workers. Everyone gets the same wage regardless of how long he worked. Some exegetes stress the
stroke of good luck that would represent for those who had sat
all day without being able to find work. But the owner does not
offer "social justice" or "human need" as a rationale for his
unusual action. He insists that he has been fair to the com-
plainers and furthermore has a right to do what he wants.

These examples illustrate the dynamics of Jesus' parables. Most of them use story lines, characters, and images that are recognizable in the everyday lives of Jesus' audience. Because the characters are like the human beings one meets in everyday life, they should not be treated as though everything they say and do is a literal image of how God responds to human beings. God does not become angry at those who refuse the invitation to salvation as the man in the great banquet does. The vineyard owner is not God, giving out a heavenly reward. He is a recognizable local farmer or grower. Some people think he is even following the advice of agricultural treatises: Use as little hired labor as possible. He can get away with that practice because there is a labor surplus, something quite unusual at harvest time. But in the end all the workers rightly receive the day's wage they would need to survive. God's Rule is not found in the grumbling, competition, and comparison that people usually engage in when they make claims about what is fair or just. The Kingdom is experienced when owners behave like this man and when workers recognize the legitimacy of his deeds.

Legal Sayings: The Challenge of Going beyond the Law

The understanding of what is right in human relationships found in parables like these dealing with the prodigal son and the vineyard owner and workers prepares us for the way in which Jesus responds to questions about the Law. He does not accept the kind of reasoning that tries to measure out rewards and punishments. He does not accept calculations based on different circumstances so that every part of the Law has thousands of rulings explaining when it does and does not apply. He does not accept the view that what is legal represents the sum total of morality – the attitude we often encounter when people assume that "if it's legal, it's okay to do."

Instead of giving legal rulings, Jesus asks the audience to

seek to live as God intends. The Law cannot specify what such a life means since the Law must prohibit or require the same actions of everyone everywhere. When the general rule becomes impossible, the Law then creates exceptions or a hierarchy in which one law overrides another. Interpreting the Law soon becomes a full-time occupation for trained scribes. But Jesus thinks that everyone can understand how God intends us to live. Everyone can understand responding to human need, generosity, compassion, justice, and the like. Everyone can learn to be honest in their dealings with others so that there is no need for elaborate contracts or "testimony under oath" with associated perjury charges. People should learn to settle their disagreements and be reconciled with others by themselves, not dragging each other into court.

This attitude toward the Law is expressed in Matthew 5:21– 48. In this section of the Sermon on the Mount, Jesus presents as inadequate such normal legal statutes as prohibition of murder (vv. 21–6), prohibition of adultery (vv. 27–30), regulations for divorce (vv. 31–2), guaranteeing one's word by swearing an oath (vv. 33–7), protection against abuse by giving people legal forms of retaliation (vv. 38–42), and finally, all the distinctions we make between persons who are friends and those who are enemies (vv. 43–8). Instead of more laws, Jesus calls for a change in the human heart that generates the kind of behavior the Law then seeks to regulate. People have argued for centuries about whether or not Jesus was being realistic in warning against anger and lust, in insisting that the only way to overcome evil is not to resist the evils others try to do us. Jesus does not claim to describe the behavior of average human beings, the kind of behavior that the wisdom teachers often characterized as folly. Jesus insists that God's own example of goodness and perfection should serve as the standard for what is good in relationships between humans. He argues that if people lived from such a "pure heart" or devotion to goodness, then the complex Law would not be necessary. That does not mean that Jesus thought the Law was a bad thing, but it could not make someone into an obedient, faithful disciple.

Today people often praise Jesus for placing human needs above the rules for keeping the Sabbath holy by refraining from all work except the greatest emergencies (e.g., Mk 2:23–3:6). They agree that inner goodness is much more important than rules about purification rituals and which foods may be eaten with other foods (e.g., Mark 7:1–8, 14–23). They might even assent to criticizing a Pharisaic custom of dedicating certain property to God so that it cannot be touched for other uses such as the obligation to provide financial support for aging parents (Mk 7:9–13). But they draw the line when it comes to Jesus' rejection of divorce (e.g., Mk 10:2–12). Jesus was not the only Jewish teacher who pointed to Genesis as evidence that God had intended lifelong marriage to one spouse. It is important to recognize that Jesus' comment does not take the form of legal ruling. He refuses to engage in determining conditions for divorce. Instead he rejects that effort by saying that the provision for divorce is found in Deuteronomy 24:1–4 because humans are "hard-hearted" (Mt 19:7–8). In this example, Jesus rejects a particular provision of the Law on the grounds that it does not represent the intentions of God, who is both creator and the real source of the Law. Moses made the provision about divorce to deal with people who persistently turn away from God to follow their own desires.

Jesus hopes his disciples will live on the basis of what God made humanity to be. We know by his openness to all who came to him that Jesus would not have rejected divorced persons. But Jesus lived in a world where ties of affection between husbands and wives were very weak. Divorce could easily be obtained. Many people had marriage contracts worked out between the bride's father, since she was often a teenager at the time of the marital agreement, and her prospective husband. In it was specified the property that was to be returned to her if a divorce occurred. Women without such contracts or a father or male relative to help her enforce them would be left helpless. (Children were presumed to belong to their father. Situations in which a woman had children from a prior marriage occurred only if she was widowed.)

Jesus directs his words to men (Mt 5:31–2), though Mark 10:12 acknowledges that in Jesus' day a wife might also leave her husband. He would have surprised an audience that assumed that divorce was a male's right when he pointed to the damage done to the wife by a husband's action: "A man who divorces his wife, makes her an adulteress." If she had enough property of her own, a woman might not remarry, but most women would have to do so to survive. In this example, Jesus points to an evil that results from a practice most people in his time considered perfectly legal. Today, we may feel that "making her an adulteress" hardly describes the injury of divorce. Instead, we could easily point to the findings of social scientists regarding the negative results of divorce for the economic and psychological well-being of the majority of divorced women and their children.

In all of these examples Jesus challenges us to do and be more than the Law could ever legislate. We are not trying to check off our behavior against a list of rules, old or new. We are trying to live with each other as God intends. The presence of God's Reign overcomes the "hard hearts" that are the basis of much of our complex legal dealings with one another.

Prophetic Sayings and Apocalyptic Images: The Reign Is Present

People in Jesus' day often imagined that the Reign of God would come soon with a great victory over all the evil nations. Some Jewish writings of the period picture earthly empires as the embodiment of cosmic forces that opposed God. Myths of the rebellious angels who were cast out of heaven and came to pollute the earth by afflicting human beings with lust, passions for luxury goods, violence, and bloodshed were used to explain the origins of the evils that humans experienced. The real battle was not against earthly empires but took place instead between God's heavenly armies and the demonic powers. In the Book of Daniel, for example, the archangel Michael is the defender of Israel (Dn 12). Prophecies and symbolic visions like those in Daniel 7–12 described the past overthrow of mighty empires, the eventual fall of the last empire, and the final judgment in which those who had remained faithful to God would be exalted. The resurrection promised the wise persons who had taught the people in the turmoil of the last times in Daniel 12:3 assures that they will shine like stars – that is, that they will become part of the heavenly world of the angels.

People who heard Jesus speaking about the Reign of God may have expected that he would describe the signs of a world coming to an end, as well as the faithfulness that righteous people have to show as the powers of evil made their last stand against God, followed by the glorious victory of God's power over evil, the judgment of the wicked, and the reward awaiting the righteous. Some Jewish writings from the period expect the righteous to play a role in the final battle against evil. Others think of the righteous as a small group of witnesses who suffer the evils of the present age until God's victory delivers them.

Some of Jesus' sayings about the Kingdom take the form of prophetic oracles. He announced that the Reign of God is at hand (Mk 1:15; Mt 10:7–8a); predicted that there are people "standing here who will not taste death before they see that the kingdom of God has come with power" (Mk 9:1); and used the budding of a fig tree as a sign for the nearness of the Kingdom (Mk 13:28–31).

Jewish writings sometimes describe the future blessings of

the new age in which God would rule over or dwell with a righteous humanity in terms of a new Jerusalem or a new temple that would replace the present city. Some Jews, like the Essenes, thought the Temple was defiled because the priests serving there were not from a legitimate line and did not observe the correct calendar or the appropriate rules of purity. At his trial, Jesus was alleged to have prophesied that the Temple would be destroyed (Mk 14:58; 15:29b–30), and his accusers said that he sought to destroy the Temple. If that had been true, then Jesus' message about the Kingdom would have suggested that his followers take direct action to bring in the Reign of God. Mark 13:2 preserves a different saying about the Temple. Jesus does not make himself the agent of its destruction, but he predicts that its magnificent buildings will be completely destroyed.

Was the Temple's destruction a sign that the end of the world was near? Mark, who may have written his Gospel during the revolt of the Jews against Rome (which led to the complete destruction of the Temple), includes a series of warnings against being led astray by "false prophets and messiahs" (Mk 13:5b–8, 19–22) in the chapter that begins with Jesus' prediction that the Temple is to be destroyed. Lest Christians think the end of the world is near, Mark concludes this chapter with the reminder that no one, not even Jesus, knows when the end will come (Mk 13:32).

Did Jesus' teaching about the Reign of God promise his followers that this world would soon come to an end, that evil would be destroyed, and that his followers would share the Kingdom with him? Some of Jesus' sayings could certainly have been understood in that way, but Mark 13's presentation of Jesus' message about the end of all things seeks to counter such expectations.

We can also find evidence in Jesus' use of imagery associated by Jewish writings with the coming judgment to suggest that he did not use images of the Reign of God and judgment in the same way as his contemporaries. The Gospels contain many references to the coming of the "Son of man" in glory or judgment (e.g., Lk 9:2b//Mt 16:27//Mk 8:38; Lk 11:30; 12:8//Mt 10:32 [replaces the reference to the "Son of man" with "I"]; Lk 12:40; Lk 17:22, 24, 26, 30//Mt 24:26–41; Lk 18:8; Lk 21:27//Mt 24:30; Lk 21:36; Lk 22:69//Mk 14:62//Mt 26:64). Scholars think Jesus might have been alluding to the vision of a figure "like a Son of man" who ascends to God's throne as the sign that the kingdoms of the earth have been destroyed and God is now ruler of the people (see Dn 7:13–14). This human figure who has ascended to the divine throne is promised an everlasting kingdom (Dn 7:14). Daniel 7:22 gives the Kingdom to the righteous, the "saints of the Most High."

Daniel seems to have identified the "Son of man" with the righteous who have suffered for their faithfulness. They will inherit the Kingdom (Dn 7:18). The link between the heavenly "Son of man" whose exaltation heralds the end of this age and the suffering of the righteous may have been the background for Jesus' predictions of his own suffering in sayings about the fate of the "Son of man." The "Son of man" must suffer (e.g., Lk 9:22//Mk 8:31//Mt 16:21 [replaces the expression "Son of man" with "I"]; Lk 9:44//Mt 17:22//Mk 9:31; Lk 18:31//Mt 20:18//Mk 10:33; Lk 22:22). Daniel separates the "Son of man," an angelic and exalted heavenly figure, from the suffering, righteous on earth, whose fate is linked with the ascent of their heavenly representative to God's throne. The Gospels place Jesus' sayings about the suffering "Son of man" in contexts that suggest that the disciples anticipate that when Jesus reaches Jerusalem, he will receive power and authority as the anointed agent of God. The certainty of judgment and vindication of Jesus' ministry expressed by the Son of man sayings that refer to the future needs to be modified by the conviction that the only way to such glory is through suffering. This perspective also informs the promises to the lowly and to those who suffer for righteousness and for the sake of the gospel found in the Beatitudes (Mt 5:3–12).

Other sayings of Jesus suggest other ways in which he changed prophetic and apocalyptic traditions as much as he did our understanding of the Law. Jesus points to the concrete activities of his own ministry – his healings and exorcisms – as signs that the power of Satan is being broken up by the presence of the Kingdom (e.g., Lk 11:20). Scholars suggest that the phrase "finger of God" is an allusion to two passages: (1) In Exodus 8:15, the third plague, which the Egyptian magicians cannot duplicate, is ascribed to the "finger of God"; (2) in Exodus 31:18, it is the "finger" by which God writes on the tablets of the Law. Thus the expression conjures up God's intervention in creating and guiding the people of Israel. It may also imply that those who thought Jesus' exorcisms were demonic in origin were "hard-hearted" like Pharaoh. They failed to heed the "sign" that God has worked. The great events of the exodus lay in the distant past; the manifestation of God's Rule was foreseen in the cosmic upheaval of an equally "mythic" future. Suddenly Jesus brings both images together. God's great saving power is to be experienced in the present.

Another Kingdom saying in which Jesus shatters expectations about the coming end of the world is Luke 17:20–1. It establishes a contrast between "coming with signs to be observed" and an unusual Greek expression *entos hymin*, which has been translated as "within you," "among you," or "within your reach." The verb translated as "observed" refers to watching the heavens for astronomical signs or to watching for apocalyptic signs of the divinely determined timetable that would lead to the end (Wis 8:8; 1 Thes 5:1; Mk 13:32). The most likely meaning for the unusual preposition *entos* is "among" or "within your reach," that is, something one can grasp. Some scholars think that the papyri texts on which the definition "within reach" is based really refer to something that is "at one's home." Jesus' saying pictures people foolishly looking in the heavens for signs or trying to decipher symbolic prophecies about the course of history when the Kingdom is "right there."

Those who sought "signs" in the heavens or in history expected a final dramatic manifestation of God's Rule after which there would be no more evil. When Jesus spoke of the Kingdom as something that could be experienced, they must have wondered how the Reign of God could be present in a world that had not been transformed? They might even have pointed to the sufferings of good people as evidence that the world was still subject to evil powers. One of Jesus' most puzzling Kingdom sayings, Matthew 11:12, suggests that failure and even violence against "the Kingdom" are possibilities: "And from the days of John the Baptist until now, the kingdom of heaven suffers violence and violent men plunder it." Jesus may have been alluding to Herod's murder of the Baptist as "plundering" the Kingdom. But, as Jesus' other sayings on suffering also suggest, this type of violence is not really a victory for "men of violence."

If Jesus changes normal apocalyptic views of the suffering of the righteous so that it is not part of a world that is increasingly ruled by evil, then we must look to other sayings to suggest how the suffering righteous prove the powerlessness of evil. The sayings against retaliation and the ethic of "love of enemy" discussed in our treatment of Jesus' understanding of the Law (Mt 5:38–48) provide a clue. The righteous person conquers evil by always responding with the compassion of God, rather than by using verbal, physical, or legal means to defend against evil.

Jesus' way of speaking about the Reign of God includes such present experiences of evil being met with love and mercy rather than hate and violence. Jesus also points to a future in which God vindicates those like the Baptist and himself who have embodied the reign. Jesus' disciples are not simply in a "holding pattern" waiting for God's Rule to be established in the future; they are already part of the Kingdom coming among humans. God does not have to destroy all the wicked on earth in order to reign among the faithful. God does not have to come with the violence of the warrior and angelic armies to break into the human world.

Jesus' revision of common apocalyptic views about the control that evil exercises over the world and the way in which God's Reign comes among humans provides support for Jesus' ethical vision. Many who sought to obey the precepts of the Law with such care were attempting to lead lives of purity and holiness in a world that was dominated by evil people and powers. Many felt that the good and evil angelic powers even waged their warfare in the hearts of human beings. Without the safeguard of the Law, humanity would be completely lost to evil. Jesus rejects their view of the Law because he rejects the notion that humans are to be regarded as evil. Jesus' parables make it evident that he is well aware of how much evil and scheming human beings are capable of, but there is another power, that of God, which can lead to actions that are quite different from the evil, hard-hearted, or blindly foolish behavior people expect of others. It is this other type of behavior that makes present experiences of the Kingdom possible for Jesus' disciples.

Much of Jesus' teaching challenges the imagination to look at the world and others differently. This new vision is not "just for the pleasure of it" as we might expect from a book or movie. We are asked to believe that the Reign of God is breaking into human affairs. Yet it is also "hidden" in the everyday stories of life. Even though it is unobserved and not a dramatic public event like the exodus, this renewed presence of God can shatter the everyday sameness of the world. People might turn their whole lives over to the Kingdom just as the merchant is willing to sell everything else to buy the really fine pearl.

Jesus challenges his audience to look beyond the Law to see what God intended humans to be. The Law can point to those intentions, but it can only partially create true justice and mercy. The Law can prohibit and punish murder, but it cannot get at the violent emotions that lead to murder in the first place. It can set up rules for oath taking and punish perjury, but it cannot make humans speak truthfully with one another. Jesus rejects our pessimistic attitudes, which say that the world is rotten and things never change. People show surprising ways of being just and merciful in the parables much as they also show the scoundrel side of human nature. Jesus also affirms the conviction at the heart of the covenant faith of Israel: God will vindicate the righteous; God is the one who seeks justice, mercy, and faith from humans.

Chapter 4

Adaptation of Jesus' Teaching in the Community

Disciples of a famous teacher expanded and interpreted their master's teaching to answer questions that arose after the master's death or to explicate unclear teaching. The lives of famous teachers were expected to reflect their doctrines. Combining episodes from a teacher's life with samples of teaching provided an effective way of passing on the views of a particular group. Frequently, biographies of famous people were framed to bring out the lessons that one could learn from the individual's life.

Scholars disagree over whether or not the Gospels should be considered biographies of Jesus, but they do agree that episodes from Jesus' life have been used to illustrate his teachings. The evangelists have also put together traditions that they inherited about Jesus in larger units, which provide interpretations for the individual sayings or stories. Sometimes when a saying or story occurs in more than one gospel it is easy to see that each writer has handled the material differently. Since early Christians believed Jesus to be the Son of man, exalted at God's right hand and coming to judge the world, an evangelist may substitute "I" for the phrase "Son of man" in a saying (e.g., Mt 16:21; contrast Mk 8:31 and Lk 9:32). We noted in the preceding chapter that Mark arranges sayings about the end of the world in Chapter 13, so that Christians will not mistake the destruction of Jerusalem as a sign of the end of the world. Since Mark emphasizes the danger posed by false prophets, the chaos and destruction of war, and the fact that Christians must expect suffering, many scholars think that the evangelist is applying sayings of Jesus to a community caught up in the uncertainties and turmoil caused by the Jewish revolt against Rome (66–70 C.E.).

In order to provide a framework for studying how the evangelists have adapted the teachings of Jesus, scholars rely on the results of three methods of analyzing gospel materials: form criticism, source criticism, and redaction criticism. We know that Jesus' deeds and teachings were handed on by word of mouth. Neither Jesus nor his immediate disciples recorded what he taught or what happened to him. Even Jesus' trial and death were not recorded at the time, as is evident from the discrepancies between the accounts and the difficulty historians have in fitting many of the details into what we know of legal practice of that time.

Form criticism identifies the individual units of material that were passed on orally such as legal and prophetic sayings, miracles, and stories of Jesus' encounters with hostile questioners. By comparing the gospel examples of these forms with each other and with other examples from the period, scholars develop a sense of the basic characteristics of each type of material as well as of the types of alterations one finds in the basic form when it appears in a longer narrative. Sometimes alterations can easily be identified because they highlight a prominent theme in the particular gospel from which the story or saying is taken.

Source criticism begins with the observation that when the three synoptic gospels, Matthew, Mark, and Luke, are compared there are major areas of agreement both in broad outlines of Jesus' ministry and in almost identical wording in particular sayings and episodes. Almost all of Mark's gospel can be found in Matthew and Luke. In episodes that they share with Mark, the verbal similarity between Matthew and Luke is greatest when they are following Mark. There is also a high degree of verbal similarity in Matthew and Luke when they have common examples of Jesus' teaching (such as the Lord's Prayer: Mt 6:9–13//Lk 11:2–4). Sometimes Mark appears to have a version of an incident different from the one being followed by Matthew and Luke (e.g., Jesus' testing in the wilderness: Mk 1:12–13; Mt 4:1–11//Lk 4:1–13).

Scholars find that the most plausible explanation for the relationships between the synoptics is the so-called two-source theory. Matthew and Luke used a written version of Mark as a framework. In addition, each had access to a written collection of Jesus' teachings, which no longer survives except in the common material preserved by Matthew and Luke. Scholars use the designation "Q" from the German word *Quelle* ("source") to designate such material. Just as Q was lost once Jesus' teaching had been incorporated into the more effective format of the gospel, scholars also agree that Mark probably had some written sources available. Perhaps there was a collection of miracles and a short collection of parables. There was probably some account of Jesus' passion and death, but it is difficult to reconstruct such sources without a second, independent parallel such as we have for the Q material.

Finally, redaction criticism draws on the results of form criticisms and source criticism to study the particularities of each Gospel. Redaction critics look for the language, themes, editorial changes, explanatory comments, and special marks of plot and structure that make each Gospel distinctive. In recent years, analysis of the overall viewpoint of individual Gospels is also being provided by exegetes who use methods derived from modern literary criticism. We will be drawing on the results of scholarly work using all of these methods as we study ways in which each Gospel presents the teaching of Jesus.

Jesus as Risen Lord

Before turning to examples of Jesus' teaching, we need to explore a fundamental difference between the Gospels and other

accounts of famous teachers. The stories of such great teachers
as Moses or Socrates or Mohammed seek to preserve the mem-
ory of persons known to be dead, though Moses and Mohammed are believed to enjoy a special place in paradise. Christians
make a very different claim about Jesus. Jesus is not dead but
lives exalted at the right hand of God (Acts 2:22–36). Jesus'
position in heaven shows that he is worthy of honor as a divine
being. The divine name "Lord" is applied to Jesus (Acts 2:35–6;
Phil 2:6–11). All of the Gospels are written out of the belief
that Jesus is more than another human teacher. He is an exalted, heavenly figure, the Son of man, the Lord, the Son of God.
Early Christians pictured Jesus interceding for them with God
(e.g., Heb 9:27–8). They also thought that Jesus' words could be
heard in the inspired speech of prophets in the Christian community (e.g., Rv 10:8–11). Therefore, Jesus is not cut off from
the community that remembers and interprets his teaching in
the same way that other teachers are. Jesus or the Holy Spirit
can still inspire new words and new understanding in the community of disciples.

The Gospel writers show us that the early Christians came
to understand Jesus' mission only after the Resurrection. They
learned to look back to the Scriptures for prophecies of the
coming of a savior who would die for the people. Luke puts the
process in narrative form concerning the events of Easter itself.
Luke 24 is divided into three major scenes: (1) Women (in Lk
24:10, Mary Magdalene, Joanna, Mary, the mother of James and
others; in Mk 16:1, Mary Magdalene, Mary, the mother of
James, and Salome; in Mt 28:1, Mary Magdalene and "the other
Mary") learn the Easter message from an angel at the empty
tomb; (2) on the road to Emmaus, two followers, Cleopas and
an unnamed companion, discover Jesus in a meal with a mysterious stranger they meet on the road; (3) Jesus reveals himself
to the disciples who have gathered together for a meal in Jerusalem. Each scene refers to the process of discovering that Jesus
is the one who fulfills the prophecies of Scripture (Lk 24:6–8,

25–7, 44–6). It is typical of Luke to build on the same topic from one scene to the next so that we have the full expression of the theme only in the final scene. In each case the "it was necessary that the Son of Man suffer" is linked to the fulfillment of the divine plan revealed in Scripture. Notice the sequence: first simply "it is necessary" (v. 7), then to fulfill Moses and the prophets (v. 26), and finally to fulfill "the law of Moses and the prophets and the Psalms" (v. 44).

Luke declares that all of the Hebrew Scriptures should be interpreted as testimony to Jesus and his destiny. The Gospels contain a number of passages from the prophets and the psalms that have been used to make the point that Jesus is the fulfillment of Scripture. Among the most famous are the passages about the suffering servant of the Lord from Isaiah 52–53 and Psalms 110:1 and 2:2, which speak of exaltation and God's Son. The suffering servant images explain Jesus' death. The psalm passages demonstrate Jesus' glory as the exalted Son of God.

Luke is not just looking for Scripture passages that refer to Jesus as the crucified one who is now exalted as the Son of God. Luke also points out that Jesus' followers had to reinterpret what they remembered of Jesus' own teaching after the Resurrection. The women are reminded of that teaching (vv. 6–7). Luke 24:44 begins with the expression, "This is what my words meant which I addressed to you while I was still with you . . ." The evangelist shows us that interpreting and understanding Jesus' teaching was a complex process in the earliest communities. It involved memories of what Jesus had said and done; it involved insights from Scripture; and it involved the conviction that the spirit of the risen Lord inspired such interpretation.

Luke 24:47 points to another important element of the post-Resurrection experience, the mission to preach the gospel. The Gospels picture Jesus sending out groups of disciples to proclaim the Reign of God. Their mission is an extension of Jesus' own healing and preaching activities. With Jesus' death and resurrection-exaltation, the disciples' preaching comes to focus on Jesus as God's agent in salvation. They do not simply repeat Jesus' sayings and parables about the Kingdom, since they have the startling news that this Jesus was God's anointed servant. He died for the sins of the people and was raised to the right hand of God. Jesus is the one who will come in judgment (e.g., 1 Thes 1:9–10; 1 Cor 15:3b–5; Rom 1:3–4). Jesus becomes the content of the gospel message. Christianity is a movement focused on the experience of Jesus as Savior, not a philosophical school for the interpretation of doctrine left by Jesus. Of course, since Jesus is still to come as judge, Christians do seek to shape their lives according to that teaching, but the authority of Jesus' teaching for Christians rests on the conviction that Jesus lives as Lord in heaven.

Luke 24:47 also points toward a major shift in early Christian preaching, the change from preaching to Israel to preaching that included the Gentiles. (The expression "the nations" was often used by Jews to refer to the Gentiles.) Even by the second half of the 50s C.E., when Paul wrote his reflections on Israel's rejection of the message about Jesus in Romans 9–11, Gentiles had come to constitute the majority in the movement.

All of the Gospels reflect a Christianity that is already well established in Gentile churches. Each evangelist has dealt with the need to make the Jewish heritage of Christianity intelligible somewhat differently in a non-Jewish community. Not surprisingly, stories in which Jesus had challenged the rigid imposition of Sabbath and purity rules have become general explanations for why the Christian communities no longer have such rules (e.g., Mark 7:1–23). The strong Jewish–Christian heritage of Matthew's community is reflected in the Gospel's emphasis on Jesus as fulfillment of the Law and the prophets (Mt 5:17–20) and limitation of the disciples' mission to the "lost sheep of Israel" (Mt 10:5). Matthew 28:16–20 invokes the authority of the risen Lord for the shift from Israel to "the nations."

It is evident in the New Testament (e.g., Gal 1–2) that Jesus' followers did not sit down in Jerusalem and work out a common mission strategy and message – indeed, conflicts divided the communities. Yet it is equally evident that the earliest Christians were convinced that their efforts were guided and mandated by the Spirit. They associated the coming of the Spirit with the resurrection–exaltation of Jesus.

The Fourth Gospel preserves a tradition about the guidance of the community by the Spirit-Paraclete (Jn 14:16–17; 14:26; 15:26; 16:7–11, 13–15). The tradition-history of these sayings is disputed. Two of them (15:26 and 16:7–11) refer to the external vindication of Jesus and his message in the face of the world's hostility and rejection. One (14:16–17) is a promise of abiding presence with the community, a promise that is also made for the dwelling of Father and Son with Christians (e.g., Jn 14:23) and of Jesus' relationship to the community in Matthew 28:20. The remaining two sayings refer to the Spirit's activity in the community process of remembering, interpreting, and applying what Jesus had said (Jn 14:26; 16:13–15).

Some of the sayings that the Gospels now attribute to Jesus in his ministry may have come from early Christian prophets speaking in the name of the risen Lord. The same saying can appear in both contexts. The risen Lord inspires the prophecy in Revelation 3:3 that he will return "like a thief." 1 Thessalonians 5:2 and 2 Peter 3:10 make the same statement as something commonly known to the reader without specifying its origin. The Gospels have this warning in the mouth of Jesus (Lk 12:39; Mt 24:43). The apocalyptic image of the Lord as "judge knocking at the door" appears in Revelation 3:20 and as an eschatological saying of Jesus in Mark 13:29 (Mt 24:33). James 5:8–9 uses this image to back up an exhortation to Christians not to grumble. The early Christians were not concerned with our distinctions between "the historical Jesus," "the risen Lord," and "general community exhortation." They understood all of these notions as guides for a life that the Lord's return in glory would vindicate before the whole world.

Jesus' Teaching in New Circumstances: Divorce

Some Christian churches treat Jesus' sayings on marriage and divorce as the starting point for systems of church law governing these matters. Roman Catholics are required to demonstrate to an ecclesiastical tribunal that there was a flaw in the marriage that prevented it from being a true, Christian marriage. They can remarry within the church only if the court finds that the previous marriage was not a marriage. Such laws attempt to respect the letter of Jesus' teaching on marriage and divorce.

Some Christians argue that the circumstances of marriage and divorce are so different in our day that Jesus' sayings cannot be turned into a rule to govern Christian behavior. Jesus himself opposed preoccupation with legal rulings. Others insist that since divorce is not part of God's intention for marriage it ought to be rigidly prohibited. No righteous person will divorce a spouse for any reason or, perhaps, for any but the most serious reason. That reason could only be the spouse's flagrant disregard for the Law as in the case of adultery, or other sexual immorality. Matthew 1:19 describes Joseph as a "just man" because although he would have to divorce his fiancée for sexual immorality, he did not seek to do so publicly.

There is no doubt that Jesus agreed with those who found the "contract to be renegotiated at will" version of marriage unacceptable. He appealed to God's intention in creating humans in two genders to demonstrate that God wanted a permanent union between husband and wife (Mk 10:2–9; Mt 19:3–9). A saying of Jesus' against divorce circulated independently of this story (Lk 16:18; Mk 10:11b; Mt 5:32; 1 Cor 7:10–11). Several versions are reflected in these examples: adaptation to non-Jewish legal formulas by which either husband or wife might be the initiating subject (Mk 10:12 makes this adaptation; 1 Cor 7:10–11 presumes it); outright condemnation (Lk 16:18; 1 Cor 7:10–11; also Mk 10:9); prohibition in all cases except *porneia* ("sexual immorality"; Mt 5:32; 19:9).

Luke 16:18 reflects the Palestinian view of the husband as the one who divorces his wife, still vaguely conceived as "his possession" (though by Jesus' time some Jewish women possessed their own property and could demand a divorce). Scholars often think that it represents the most primitive form of Jesus' saying.

The "except for sexual immorality" clause is a later addition to the tradition. Paul, writing in the early 50s C.E., does not know it. However, Luke 16:18 lacks the intensification of the moral urgency that we have seen in much of Jesus' teaching and that we find in Matthew 5:32. There, the husband is accused of "making his wife an adulteress." Instead of treating her as responsible (whether by adultery or some other reason the husband might specify to fit the "cause" required by the Law in Dt 24:1–4), Jesus' saying pictures her as the victim. The very act of a man divorcing his wife is questioned.

A peculiarity of Luke 16:18 is the assertion that marriage to a divorced person constitutes adultery. Most Jews would have said that possession of a divorce decree freed the parties from such a charge. A prohibition against a man marrying a divorced woman did exist in Palestinian Judaism, but it applied to priests who were to serve in the Temple: "They shall not marry a harlot or a woman defiled; neither shall they marry a woman divorced from her husband" (Lv 21:7; cf. Ez 44:22). Extension of rules for priestly purity to the lives of "the righteous" generally occurred among sects such as the Pharisees and the Essenes. The Essenes applied the prohibition against the king having more than one wife (Dt 17:17) to members of the sect in support of the prohibition against marrying another woman while the first wife is alive (Damascus Document 4:20–5:1). Luke 16:18 reflects a view of holiness in keeping with the legal rulings of sectarian Judaism.

The Essene legal tradition makes it possible to understand the exception, "sexual immorality" (*porneia*), in Matthew as representative of a concern for the holiness of the community. Although some translations render the Greek *porneia* as "adultery," the normal Greek for adultery is *moicheia* (its verbal form is used in Mt 5:27–28, 32). *Porneia* is a term used for "sexual immorality" of various types. It can be applied in situations in which a marriage is considered incestuous. Essene law used the Hebrew equivalent to prohibit as incestuous marriages between uncles and nieces, an addition to the prohibition of unions between aunts and nephews (in Lv 18:13). Some scholars conclude that Matthew's Jewish–Christian community expected its members to dissolve marriages that were incestuous by Jewish, though not by pagan, standards. Others point to the use of the word *porneia* as equivalent to "idolatry." This usage is based on the prophetic texts that speak of Israel's fornication with pagan gods. They suggest that this clause was added to permit Christians to dissolve a marriage to a pagan spouse. On either reading, the addition "except for *porneia*" represents an exception to the blanket prohibition of divorce aimed at safeguarding the holiness of the community. It is not an attempt to make Jesus' teaching easier.

Paul addresses the question of a Christian–pagan marriage in 1 Corinthians 7:12–16. His insistence that the believing partner makes the marriage holy (v. 14) shows that the issue of whether or not such a marriage should be dissolved stems from the conviction that a person becomes "impure" or "polluted" through illicit sexual relationships. Paul says that he does not know a saying of the Lord addressed to this situation. However, he thinks that the appropriate response is twofold: (1) The Christian is not obligated to divorce a spouse for remaining a pagan; (2) if the Christian is divorced by a spouse who is unwilling to live peacefully with a Christian, then the prohibition against marrying another person does not apply.

These examples show that Jesus' teaching was already interpreted in different ways by early Christian communities prior to the writing of the Gospels. None of the applications of Jesus' words about divorce seeks to change the evaluation of divorce that goes back to Jesus. But as soon as early Christians began to ask what sort of rules were to be derived from that teaching, they found themselves faced with cases that did not seem to fit. In all of the examples, the resolution of the cases is linked with an understanding of what holiness is. These communities are not trying to "update" Jesus by simply making Christian practice a reflection of the common behavior of the culture.

Collecting Jesus' Teaching: Q, The Sermon on the Mount, Matthew 17:22–18:35

The Gospel writers each bring together units of Jesus material. Even when Matthew and Luke are following a grouping that they have taken from Mark, they make changes in the material. For example, Mark 4:1–34 collects a group of parables to illustrate Jesus' teaching about the mystery of the Reign of God. The teaching alternates between the "crowd," who are said not to understand because Jesus speaks in parables (Mk 4:11–12), and the disciples to whom the Lord must explain everything privately (vv. 10, 34). The interpretation of the Parable of the Sower (vv. 13–20) is given only to the disciples. Sayings warning the reader that one must take care how one "hears" the word (Mk 4:21–5) connect the explanation of the Sower with the next parable, the Seed Growing of Itself (4:26–9).

Matthew 13:1–52 and Luke 8:4–18 are based on this section of Mark. All three versions open with the sequence: (1) the Parable of the Sower, (2) Jesus' words about parables and the mystery of the Kingdom, (3) the explanation of the Parable of the Sower. Matthew has moved the saying about the one who has received more from Mark 4:25 into the section on the parables and the mystery of the Kingdom (Mt 13:12). Luke retains its Marcan position. Matthew omits the rest of the sayings in Mark 4:21–4, though variants of those sayings occur elsewhere in his Gospel. Luke shortens the collection by omitting two of the proverbs (Mk 4:23 and 24bc).

Luke stops following Mark after the warning about hearing the word of God (Lk 8:18; Mk 4:24–5), in order to insert the episode about Jesus' true relatives (Lk 8:19–21). He picks up Mark again with the stilling of the storm (Lk 8:22–5; Mk 4:35–41).

Matthew, on the other hand, has continued to follow Mark but has substituted a parable, the Weeds and the Wheat (Mt 13:24–30), for Mark's Parable of the Seed Growing of Itself (Mk 4:26–9). Matthew follows the Mustard Seed (Mk 4:30–2; Mt 13:33) with the Parable of the Leaven (Mt 13:33), which is not in Mark. However, in Luke 13:20–1 we find this parable attached to the Parable of the Mustard Seed (Lk 13:18–19). Matthew appears to substitute the pair of parables from Q for the single one that he finds in Mark. Then Matthew rewrites the first part of Mark's conclusion (Mk 4:33) to show that Jesus' speaking in parables to the crowds fulfills Daniel 12:3 (Mt 13:34–5). He omits Mark 4:34 and adds more private instruction of the disciples. An explanation of the Weeds and the Wheat (Mt 13:36–43) is followed by the parables of the Treasure, the Pearls, and the Net (13:44–50). Finally Matthew concludes his parable collection with a different saying about the disciples than he found in Mark 4:34. Mark's ending suggests that the disciples had difficulty understanding Jesus' teaching.

Matthew changes the conclusion in order to show that the disciples are "scribes trained for the Reign of God" because they have understood all of Jesus' teaching (13:51–2).

The most familiar examples of reworked Q material are the Beatitudes (Lk 6:20–3//Mt 5:3–12) and the Lord's Prayer (Lk 11:2–4//Mt 6:9–13). As we have seen in its treatment of Mark 4, Matthew collects the teachings of Jesus into discourses. This feature of Matthew's composition makes the Gospel suitable for instruction within the community. Matthew has located the Beatitudes and the Lord's Prayer in the first and most famous discourse in the Gospel, the Sermon on the Mount (Mt 5:1–7:29). In addition to the discourse on parables (Chapter 13), Matthew contains three others. Each discourse includes a formal opening indicating that Jesus is beginning to instruct his disciples and a conclusion noting that he has finished speaking. The other three discourses concern the mission (Mt 10:1–11:1), relationships within the community (Mt 18:1–19:1), and the coming of the judgment (Mt 24:1–26:1).

When we study passages taken from Mark, we can easily see how each evangelist had rearranged the material. Since Q material can only be identified by the overlap between Matthew and Luke, it is more difficult to determine whether the differences between Matthean and Lucan versions of a saying or episode are all due to the editing by the evangelists or reflect differences in the edition of Jesus' teaching used by each author. Matthew's tendency to compose extended discourses makes it appear likely that when pieces of tradition appear together in Matthew, but in separate places in Luke, they were not linked together in Q.

The study of Q material plays an important role in the attempts of scholars to recover the original teaching of Jesus and to understand how it was transmitted by Christians in the forty to sixty years between the death of Jesus and the composition of the Gospels. They have advanced various hypotheses about the development of traditions about Jesus' teaching in Q material. Some have emphasized the parallels between Q and collections of sayings by other wise men. They think that the collection began to take shape around the image of Jesus as spokesperson for divine wisdom (cf. Lk 7:35; 10:21–2; 11:49–51). Others note that Q as reconstructed from Matthew and Luke has an eschatological focus. Presuming that the sequence of Q material found in Luke corresponds more nearly to the source, Q concludes with a series of five sayings on the day of the Son of man (Lk 17:23–4, 26–7, 33, 34–5, 37); the Parable of the Pounds, seen as a warning for disciples in the Lord's absence (Lk 19:13, 15b–24, 26); and a promise that the disciples will share in the banquet to come and the judgment of Israel (Lk 22:28b, 30b). This understanding of Q represents it as the teaching one must follow to be vindicated by the Son of man in the final judgment.

According to the first view, the earliest image of Jesus was that of a wisdom teacher; the apocalyptic elements were introduced by Christians who had identified Jesus with the coming Son of man. Sections of Q material emphasize the reality of judgment, while other sections represent wisdom teaching. Several clusters of prophetic words in Q condemn the "present generation," those who refuse to repent and are blind to the signs of the Kingdom's coming (Lk 3:7–9, 16–17; 7:1–10, 18–28 [16:16?]; 11:14–15, 16, 17–26, 29–32, 33–6, 39–52; 17:23–37). Other sayings are directed at the community. They explain how disciples are to act in the world (Lk 6:20–49; 11:2–4, 9–13; 12:22b–31, 33–4) and instruct those engaged in preaching the gospel (9:57–62; 10:2–16; 12:2–12). Prophetic sayings are sometimes inserted into such blocks of material. Luke 10:13–15 shifts from instructing missionaries to indicting those who reject the gospel.

Sayings that follow the patterns of wisdom teaching, even those that we now find used to emphasize judgment, originally had the focus on universal patterns of human behavior that is typical of wisdom material. Acts and their consequences are presented (Lk 6:37–8; 11:4, 9, 33), and observations are grounded in nature (6:35c; 12:6–7, 24, 26–8, 29–33). The wisdom teaching in Q may have originally been arranged in thematic units: For example, Luke 6:20–3, 27–33, 35b–6, 37a, 38b, 39bc, 40–2, 43–9 contains an inaugural speech by Jesus, which Matthew will expand in the Sermon on the Mount; Luke 9:57–60 and 10:2–12, 13–15, 16, 21–2, 23–4 focus on disciples as preachers of the gospel; Luke 12:2–9, 10, 11–12 exhorts disciples to fearless testimony, whereas Luke 12:22b–31, 33–4 urges them to be concerned with heavenly treasure, not anxious about material things. Wisdom teaching presents Jesus as the teacher-master to whom the student must listen (Lk 4:40, 46). Like other teachers of wisdom, his life-style must be imitated (Lk 9:57–8; implied in 14:26, 27; 17:33). When this picture is combined with the image of Jesus as the heavenly Son of man, Jesus' voice is no longer the timeless voice of wisdom but the prophetic summons that initiates the "harvest" of the last days – a summons carried forward into the world by his disciple–envoys (10:16). This message calls for the unqualified obedience of all who hear it.

The combination of wisdom sayings with an eschatological orientation also appears in Matthew's version of Jesus' "inaugural sermon," the Sermon on the Mount. This sermon sets out Matthew's fundamental vision of the life of discipleship, which is now possible in view of Jesus' coming as the one who fulfills the Law and the prophets (Mt 5:17). When the Gospel concludes with the instruction to teach the nations to observe what Jesus has taught (28:20), Matthew probably intends the reader to think of the Sermon on the Mount as an epitome of Jesus' teaching. It is the way in which a righteousness more abundant than that of "scribes and Pharisees" is produced

(5:20): It shows the hearer how to carry out the task of seeking the Reign of God and its righteousness before all else (5:6; 6:33).

The major divisions within the Sermon on the Mount are well marked: (1) Matthew 5:3–16, discipleship; (2) Matthew 5:17–48, more abundant righteousness in relationships with others; (3) Matthew 6:1–7:11, more abundant righteousness in single-hearted devotion to God; (4) Matthew 7:12, the Golden Rule (concluding summary); (5) Matthew 7:13–27, a warning to choose the narrow way of righteousness. Exegetes debate over details of the tradition history of the material contained in the Sermon. The parallels between Matthew and Luke suggest that the former brought together material found in the Q source. The evangelist shaped Jesus' teaching about the Law into the antitheses of Matthew 5:21–48: "You have heard it said . . . but I say to you . . ." This section is introduced by the affirmation that Jesus came not to destroy the Law but to show people a greater righteousness. In their Matthean form, the antitheses sharpen the contrast between Jesus' authoritative teaching and that of other interpreters of the Law.

When Matthew takes over wisdom material, such as the section on anxiety (Mt 6:25–34), he also uses an antithesis to distinguish the behavior of the disciples from that of other persons. The "Gentiles" are the ones who concern themselves with material goods (v. 32). Jesus' disciples must let nothing take priority over their quest for God's Reign and God's righteousness. The section itself reflects a theme common to wisdom traditions (cf. Wis 7:1–6). It also appeals to a theme common in the preaching of the Cynics that anxiety has been created by human culture. Instead of being willing to live "naturally," with what is provided for us by nature just as animals are provided for, humans engage in activities designed to satisfy artificial needs. The process of agriculture – sowing, reaping, and gathering into barns – serves as an example of false anxieties. The hearer is told to have confidence in the beneficence that God shows throughout creation. Matthew 6:33 shifts from the wisdom perspective as well as that of the Cynics by emphasizing the one "anxiety" a disciple ought to show, namely, for the righteousness appropriate to the Reign of God.

The sharp contrasts in righteousness that set the disciples of Jesus over against others, scribes, and Pharisees in Matthew 5:20, and Gentiles in 6:32, create difficulties for Christian readers today who are sensitive to the need to respect the religious and moral traditions of others. Matthew often directs very harsh words at Jewish religious teachers. In order to understand these criticisms in their context, we need to remember that Matthew's community has a strong Jewish–Christian heritage. We have already seen that Matthew's handling of the divorce saying establishes a holiness for Christian marriage that follows some Jewish traditions about appropriate and inappropriate marriages. Matthew does not reject the fundamental insights about righteousness that have come from the community's Jewish heritage.

Matthew 23:2–3 even commends some of the teaching of those who are "on Moses' seat." But the reader is quickly warned against their example: one that creates burdens and excludes people from the Kingdom. The section satirizes hypocritical teaching among the scribes and Pharisees. The satire has all too often been used to justify Christian distortions of Jewish piety as have the associated warnings against hypocritical piety in the Sermon on the Mount. But one should note the function of the satire in both cases. Matthew is drawing guidelines for a Christian community that could easily recreate in itself the practices and distinctions being condemned. The warning against copying the external marks of righteousness, the titles, and seeking the public honor paid to the scribes and teachers of the Law (23:5–12) makes this point clearly. Start down that road, this sharply drawn satire warns, and one will end up losing the Reign of God and even persecuting God's messengers.

The Sermon on the Mount also includes warnings directed toward the community. Its members are to remain "separate" from two other groups: (1) the "hypocrites" and others who practice the righteousness of scribes and Pharisees; and (2) the Gentiles who are pictured as totally lacking in piety (5:47; 6:7–8, 32). But there are also warnings against those within the community whose lives do not produce the "good fruit" required of them (7:15–23). The example of wise and foolish housebuilders serves as a concluding warning that it is necessary to both hear and do Jesus' word (7:24–27). The sayings on "false prophets," those who call on Jesus but will not be acknowledged by him, show that the demand to separate oneself from the behavior of a Jewish community that follows scribal interpretation of the Law and from an irreligious gentile population does not pretend to create a community of the perfect among Christians. Christians too are subject to judgment. Even some of those who are community leaders, prophets, and healers could be found lacking.

The comments about true and hypocritical piety in Matthew 6:1–18 must also address dangers within the Christian community. As in Judaism, prayer, almsgiving, and fasting represent the foundations of piety in Matthew's community. Jesus' coming as the one who "fulfills" the Law and the prophets has also changed the way in which disciples meet those obligations toward God. Matthew draws a contrast between external behavior, observed and evaluated by others, and true devotion to God. Just as true righteousness in keeping the Law looked only to God for its understanding of how humans should relate to one another, so the truly religious person seeks only the praise that comes from God. The section on anxiety and divine providence promises the disciples that they can rely on God's concern for them to provide what is needed to live such a life.

The Sermon on the Mount alludes to several areas in which tensions will arise within the community: the divisions caused by anger and the refusal to forgive others (5:21–6; 6:14–15; 7:1–2); self-exaltation and disdain for others by persons who claim to possess righteousness (6:1–6, 16–18; 7:3–5); and false teachers, able to deceive under the guise of Christianity (7:15, 21–3). These problems are more directly addressed in the discourse on relationships within the community (Mt 18:1–19:1). Once again Matthew has drawn together traditional material into a discourse that will speak to the specific problems the community is facing.

Immediately before the discourse, Matthew relates an episode in which Jesus resolves the question of whether his followers should pay the tax demanded of Jewish males for the support of the Temple (Mt 17:24–7). Peter is the one who must obtain an answer from his master about the tax question in response to the Jewish authorities. Later in the discourse Peter again asks Jesus for an authoritative statement on the extent to which Christians are bound to forgive others (18:21–2). Matthew uses the Temple tax episode to establish Peter as one to whom others can turn to receive an authoritative interpretation of the meaning of Jesus' teaching.

The Temple tax episode may represent a conflict of conscience that arose for Jewish members of Matthew's community, the type of situation that made new interpretations of Jesus' teaching necessary. After the Jewish revolt in 70 C.E., the Romans expanded the half-shekel tax (a shekel is a unit of currency used among Jews) that Jewish males had previously sent to support the Temple by demanding that the tax be paid to a fund at Rome and that payment be collected for all members of a household, including slaves. Officials from the local Jewish community were responsible for making the collection. Documents from the end of the first century indicate that the Romans also sought to enforce collection from persons who "falsely" claimed that they were not Jewish. The Jewish Christians of Matthew's church would have been in just such a bind. The community is separated from the synagogues of the scribes and Pharisees. Matthew even emphasizes the distinctiveness of Christians over against such persons. The story affirms that the "sons" (Christians) are indeed "free" but demonstrates a willingness to pay anyway in order not to "scandalize" them. Jewish Christians are willingly participating in the suffering of their fellow Jews. At the same time, the story emphasizes that this gesture does not surrender the Christian's freedom.

The discourse that follows the Temple tax incident is addressed to leaders of the community. Matthew 18:1–14 spells out the kind of humility that is required of those who are children of the one heavenly Father. The images used in this section portray "becoming like a child" in order to enter the Kingdom as accepting and not scandalizing the "little ones" – a task Jesus' disciples cannot neglect. Matthew appears to use the expression "little ones" both as a designation for Christians in general (as he does in 25:40, 45) and to refer to marginal persons within the Christian community whom its leaders might neglect or despise (18:6, 10, 14). Verses 6–7 recognize that as long as this world has not been transformed by the Lord's coming, scandal, temptation, and sin will occur. But that does not excuse laxity or cynicism. Verses 6–9 suggest that some of the "little ones" may go astray as a result of the scandal created by others, the teachers and evildoers of Matthew 7:15–23. One should be willing to suffer any physical horror rather than introduce evils among the "little ones" of the community. This use of an image of willingness to sacrifice a hand or an eye rather than to commit sin was also used in the Sermon on the Mount (Mt 5:29–30).

Verses 10–14 use the Parable of the Lost Sheep (which Mt took from Q; see Lk 15:2–7) to demonstrate the proper response to a "little one" who has strayed. Matthew's framework (vv. 10, 14) recalls the liturgical language of the Lord's Prayer by referring to the "will of your Father who is in heaven" (v. 14; cf. Mt 6:8–10). The image of a searching shepherd recalls a passage from the Hebrew prophet Ezekiel. God is pictured as the one who will bring back a people who have been led astray by leaders who are evil shepherds (Ez 34:11–12, 16). Jesus' parable focuses on individuals rather than the nation of Israel (i.e., a flock of sheep). It pictures a shepherd leaving the rest of the flock "on the mountains" to search for a stray one (v. 12). Matthew's version of the parable differs from Luke's in its report on the conclusion of the search. In Matthew (v. 13), the success or failure of the search is not certain. Luke 15:4–5 presumes that the lost sheep is found and uses that as the cause for joyous celebration. Since joyous celebration over the repentance of sinners is a typical Lucan theme, many scholars think that Matthew's version better represents the Q version.

Verses 15–20 introduce directions for individual and community action for dealing with a fellow Christian who has strayed. Similar community rules have been found among the writings of the Essenes. Evidence that a fellow member is sinning must be brought to the overseer of the community by appropriate witnesses. Those who continue to resist correction may be expelled from the community. Matthew also contains rules for obtaining suitable witnesses to an offense, a procedure for bringing the dispute before the church, and the expulsion of persons who will not accept decisions of the community (v. 17). The real consequences of being expelled from the community are elaborated in verses 18–20. Such a person is cut off from the Kingdom. This harsh conclusion only follows when a person has resisted all of the efforts made to bring one back. God desires the salvation of all the "little ones" (v. 14), not their condemnation.

These procedures show that Matthew's church has a structure for admitting and expelling members. Matthew does not, however, specify particular individuals or groups within the community charged with such regulatory activities such as we find among the Essenes. The presentation in Matthew 18 suggests that any disciple may find her- or himself as sheep or shepherd, as sinner or one seeking to bring about reconciliation. The sayings in verses 18–20 suggest that the formal reconciliation or expulsion took place in the context of communal prayer in the name of Jesus, who is externally present with the community.

The concluding section of the discourse moderates the harshness of the process of community discipline by highlighting Jesus' teaching on forgiveness (18:21–35). The instructions on prayer in the Sermon on the Mount (Mt 6:14–15) underscore the connection between forgiving those who offend us and being forgiven by God. In the concluding verses, Peter's question (vv. 21–2) and the Parable of the Unforgiving Servant (vv. 23–34) make it clear that there is no limit to forgiveness. The dramatic asymmetry in the amounts owed when adapted to the Matthean parallel makes the small amounts that humans forgive "insignificant." The concluding exhortation parallels the solemn ending of the Parable of the Lost Sheep (v. 14). It also emphasizes the characteristic of true righteousness throughout the gospel. It must come "from the heart."

These examples from Matthew show that the evangelist consistently shapes inherited traditions about Jesus' teaching to address the needs of a Christian community for instruction about how Christians are to relate to problems posed by the hostility of outsiders as well as problems posed by persons within the community. Jesus is the one who makes the higher righteousness of God's Reign possible. We have seen that words were not the only thing a teacher passed on to disciples. The teacher also provided a living example of the teaching. This discourse opened with sayings about the humility appropriate to Jesus' followers. Later, Matthew contrasts Christian leaders as humble servants with others who seek their own glory (23:8–12). The supreme example of the humble one who is exalted is that of Jesus, the Son of man handed over to death but raised on the third day (Mt 17:22–3). Jesus is not only the one who shows people how to live for the Reign of God; he is also the one who brings salvation to the nations by suffering as God's servant (Mt 12:15–21). Matthew 9:36–8 pictures Jesus looking with compassion upon the people, who are as lost as sheep without a shepherd, and asking God to send more laborers to help with the harvest. Although Matthew's discourses place great emphasis on the teaching of Jesus and the necessity to shape one's life in accord with those teachings or be condemned in the judgment, the gospel does not lose sight of the love and compassion for humanity that was the foundation of Jesus' teaching and his death on the cross. Matthew 28:16–20 instructs Jesus' disciples, whom the Sermon on the Mount refers to as the light of the world (Mt 5:13–16) to spread that message to all people.

Chapter 5

Characteristic Themes
in Jesus' Teaching

We have already treated the central image in Jesus' preaching, the Reign of God. Jesus spoke of the hopes that many people had for a judgment that would finally destroy all evil and permit the righteous the peace and joy in God's presence that goodness deserved. He taught that God's presence could be experienced even in this world if people would live with mercy and compassion, if they would learn to rely on God's goodness rather than on human systems of power. Jesus did not promise that such a life would lead to riches and success on earth. His own life demonstrated that humility and suffering were part of a life dedicated to God (e.g., Mt 5:3–11).

Jesus used images like that of the heavenly Son of man to reassure his followers that success in God's eyes could not be measured by human standards. God's own judgment would vindicate everything Jesus did and taught. The early Christians experienced the truth of Jesus' vision of God when they learned that Jesus' humiliation on the cross had been turned into heavenly glory at the right hand of God. This conviction meant that Jesus' words had the authority of divine revelation behind them.

In this final chapter, we are going to survey some of the other themes of Jesus' teaching that are particularly important for Christians today. The theme of *justice and solidarity* is especially prominent in social ethics and liberation theologies from Third World countries. The problem of bringing about justice in a corrupt world is understood to require that people overcome the divisions that separate and create hostility between different groups. The theme of *wealth and "the rich"* emerges not only in liberation theologies, it is also of concern to churches in developed countries. On the one hand, wealth appears to generate false values that drive people away from God and from the poor and disadvantaged who need their help. On the other hand, Christians who have wealth can use it to contribute to the well-being of the whole community. The theme of *forgiveness* embraces many dimensions of Christian life. It is the basis for a Christian's relationship to God. It also governs the way in which Christians are to respond to injuries that they suffer from others. The theme of *prayer* speaks of the way in which Christians maintain their relationship with God. In this section, we will take a detailed look at the central prayer of all Christians, the Lord's Prayer. The theme of *love of one's enemies* brings us to the heart of what Jesus meant in speaking about love. Many people find it the most unbelievable of all of Jesus' teachings. We have been conditioned by centuries of human development to separate our world into friends and enemies and to respond accordingly to each group. In some situations, this distinction is a matter of life or death. With his customary shock to our imagination, Jesus tells a story of a situation of one person's willingness to treat an enemy as though he were a friend, the Parable of the Good Samaritan. This type of love is the fulfillment of everything Jesus had to teach.

Justice and Solidarity

Jesus' audience lived in a world that seemed to be dominated by evil and injustice. The Jews were a conquered people forced to live at the whim of the Romans and the Herodian monarchs who served as client kings of the Roman Empire. Most people also lived in dependence on absentee landlords, their stewards, or wealthy persons in the local community. There was little freedom in such a world. Only the wealthy with ties to Herod's court or to the Romans had power and authority. When Jesus mentions kings, wealthy people, or landlords and stewards in his parables, he always looks at them from the perspective of the villager or artisan who was dependent on their goodwill. Jesus does not speak as though he were an "equal" in the world of the Roman ruler, the Herodian courtier, or the priestly aristocracy. He is not. Like John the Baptist, Jesus is able to spread his message as God's word without gaining the patronage of someone from the circles of power because Judaism had a tradition going back to the earliest prophets and kings in which God might select an obscure person to receive the Spirit and carry a message to the people. Most of the great prophets in the Old Testament did not come from the official circles of professional prophets. Israel's greatest king, David, was chosen to rule even though he was only a young shepherd boy at the time God sent the prophet Samuel to anoint him.

In the Old Testament, the prophets usually directed their preaching to the priests, kings, and aristocratic leaders of society. The repentance and conversion of the leaders of the people would be necessary for the nation to be renewed. By the time of Jesus, many people had come to suspect the powerful members of society as hopelessly enmeshed in evil. If they could not be converted, then the only solution was to wait for them to be overthrown at the end of the world. Jesus takes a very different approach. He announces God's Reign among the masses of people who were without status, power, or authority.

The opening speeches in both Matthew (5:3–12) and Luke (4:16–19) announce that the prophetic promise of salvation for the poor, the sick, the oppressed is being fulfilled. The Q form of the Beatitudes, which scholars believe have been expanded in Matthew's version (Mt 5:3–12//Lk 6:20–3), speaks directly of this reversal of the fate of those suffering in the land (reconstructed from Lk 6:20–1):

> Blessed the poor, for the Kingdom of God is theirs.
> Blessed the hungry, for they shall be filled.
> Blessed those who weep, for [they shall rejoice].

The Beatitudes were then expanded with the beatitude of the persecuted disciples (Lk 6:22–3). Matthew 5:3 adds the expression "in spirit" after "poor" in the opening beatitude. This addition does not mean to lessen the message that the poor are blessed in the Kingdom. But Matthew wants to make it clear that "poor" does not refer simply to a condition of material deprivation. It refers to those who are the "poor righteous," the *anawim* or "little ones." Such persons are powerless and poor in this world because they will not make the compromises with evil required to attain wealth and power. They will remain faithful to God's Law even in the face of suffering because they expect that God will deliver them. The tradition behind the Magnificat (Lk 1:46–55) expresses the piety and hopes of such groups.

What is the "good news to the poor" (Is 61:1) that has been fulfilled in Jesus? Certainly poverty, hunger, and suffering have not been erased from human history and will always require human charity (cf. Mk 14:7). None of those who were victimizing the people – the Romans, the Herodians, the wealthy landowners, and so on – were physically overthrown by Jesus. The Jewish revolt in 66–70 C.E. demonstrated how futile such an attempt would have been. Many of the "pious" had been disillusioned by the more successful revolt of the Maccabees in the second century B.C.E. Although this revolt against the Seleucid kings and corruption of the people by Greek ways claimed to restore God's rule over the people, the Hasmonean kings became as corrupt as those they replaced. Their alliances with Rome eventually paved the way for the subjection of the Jewish nation to Rome. Some of Jesus' own followers may have thought that God would use Jesus to be the instrument of another political upheaval. That was the charge for which the Romans executed him. Yet nothing in Jesus' behavior or teaching supports that interpretation of his intentions.

What then is the "good news"? Social psychologists and the experiences of Christians in Third World countries can help us understand how Jesus' teaching represented good news for the poor. Poverty and oppression have an impact on the minds of their victims just as much as they do on those who benefit from the system. Victims blame themselves for their situation. If they were "worthy," God would have placed them among the rich and powerful. We can already see that everything in Jesus' teaching and practice challenges this mentality. As we saw in the Parable of the Lost Sheep, no person is "worthless" before God. God does not seek the loss or suffering of anyone.

Another element of poverty, oppression, or powerlessness is an increase in violence, hostility, and resentment among the sufferers themselves. Tensions that cannot be expressed against one's masters break out in other forms. We cannot miss the fact that there is a great deal of conflict and tension in Jesus' parables. The unforgiving servant is one example. He is used to subjection to a powerful king and takes out his frustration at his personal subjection on others lower than he. Everyone in Jesus' world had to deal with such "officials." But the result in this case is that the servant is unchanged when the king behaves in a totally unexpected way and forgives the huge debt. The servant goes out and attacks another who owes him a small debt. The final result of his failure to change is that the king turns back into the powerful potentate and sends the unforgiving servant off to be tortured in jail (Mt 18:23–34).

Jesus takes another example of day laborers in a vineyard who become enraged when the owner pays everyone a day's wage regardless of the length of time worked (Mt 20:1–15). Although not so dramatic as the Parable of the Unforgiving Servant, this parable too addresses a problem created by injustice and violence "in the system": People become so corrupted that they can only relate to others in those terms. As a result even extraordinary acts of generosity by those who have the resources to forgive a debt or assist a laborer whose family might starve without harvest-time work can be ineffective. Justice requires something more than the redistribution of assets. It requires a conversion in the way people deal with others. That is why some scholars have seen the Parable of the Vineyard Workers as a lesson in human solidarity. The workers must surrender thinking of the landowner as the "enemy" and of themselves as engaged in an individual struggle to compete with everyone else. When this parable is connected with the other sayings of Jesus about "greatness and service," it undercuts any claim to privilege because of how much one has done for the "little ones." Unless we overcome such false perceptions, our justice will not reflect that of God.

Wealth and "the Rich" in the Teaching of Jesus

The theme of wealth and "the poor" appears frequently in the teaching of Jesus. It is especially prominent in Luke's Gospel. We have seen that the gospel message to the poor gives them "worth" in God's eyes. They are not invisible. We have also seen that Jesus and his followers live in a way that places them among the poor. They are radically dependent on others. They have had to abandon whatever little security they could have gained through farming, fishing, and other trades to follow Jesus. Jesus does not permit them to enrich themselves by charging fees for teaching. They must depend entirely on the hospitality that others are willing to offer.

We have seen that Jesus recognized the anxieties created by such dependence. Yet a number of sayings suggest that even worse is the alternative, the anxieties and blindness generated in pursuit of wealth (e.g., Mt 6:19–21, 24; Mk 10:25, 28–30).

Two parables dramatize this fact. The Parable of the Rich Fool (Lk 12:16–21) is appended to an episode in which Jesus refuses to intervene in a dispute over inheritance (Lk 12:13–15). The fool's only solution to the luck of getting a superabundant harvest is to build even bigger grain elevators to store his wheat. Where does such greed get him? Nowhere. Death intervenes before he can enjoy this wealth. The Parable of the Rich Man and Lazarus (Lk 16:19–31) dramatizes the hard-heartedness of the rich. Not only is this man completely insensitive to the Law (which requires that the rich aid the poor in life), he is still trying to order Lazarus around and receive favors for himself in hell! This parable suggests that the rich have enough teaching about how they are to use their wealth in the Law. Those who do not listen to that will not listen to anything else. But in the end the poor sufferer is vindicated and the rich man condemned.

Jesus told another parable about a lazy but clever steward who avoided disaster by reducing the accounts of what his master's debtors owed him (Lk 16:1–8a). This story would not have evoked any sympathy for either the absentee master or the steward in Jesus' audience. But some who heard Jesus may have been in situations like that of the debtors where they had had to borrow seed for planting from the steward of a wealthy man. Despite prohibitions in the Law against taking interest from a fellow Israelite, interest was collected. The loan was simply written up to include the interest in the amount borrowed. This steward, who is about to be fired for "wasting" his master's goods, turns around and ensures that someone will take him in by reducing or canceling the interest. Jesus did not approve of the impoverishment of persons by the systems of debt and interest that existed in his day (e.g., Mt 5:42). He certainly does not think that clever manipulation of the system is an end in itself. But this parable is a lesson in the shrewdness that confronts one. Luke has appended a number of sayings that apply the parable to the disciple's attitude toward wealth. One must beware of being taken in by greed.

Clearly there are two strains in the teaching of Jesus. One speaks of a radical break with wealth and the whole mentality of getting rich. The anxieties, greed, blindness, and out-and-out dishonesty required cannot be squared with the righteousness required of Jesus' disciples. For some that may be very difficult, as in the story of the rich man who wanted to become one of Jesus' disciples (Mk 10:17–22). The other speaks of the obligations of the rich toward the poor. The normal calculations of benefit or repayment cannot apply. In the Parable of the Great Banquet the poor are brought in precisely because they cannot reciprocate. They are the ones in need of the banquet and, as it turns out, the only ones who accept the invitation (Lk 14:15–24). Almsgiving and generosity that do not demand any form of repayment, not even the constant waiting on a wealthy benefactor that was typical of ancient life, are the examples Jesus gives to the rich.

Forgiveness Is for All

Luke 24:47 summarizes the content of the message that the disciples are to take to the nations as "repentance and forgiveness of sins." We have seen that Jesus included all persons in his circle of disciples. We have also seen that forgiveness was to be a fundamental characteristic of relationships between disciples. Without forgiving the offenses of others, they cannot expect forgiveness from God (Mt 6:14–15; 18:21–35).

Luke emphasizes the theme of forgiveness and joy in his gospel. We have noted that it dictated his interpretation of the Parable of the Lost Sheep (Lk 15:3–7). The most famous dramatization of this theme is the Parable of the Prodigal Son (Lk 15:11–32) in which the father's response to the return of his wayward son is to throw an extravagant banquet – just as though the young man had done something worthy of congrat-ulations. Here too we find Jesus' concern for solidarity rather than division. The elder son, dutiful and hard-working, voices the protest that many in the audience would feel. After all, the younger son was willing to come back just as a servant. Isn't this huge celebration a "slap in the face" for the good son?

Sometimes people condemn the elder son for complaining. But when we see the problem of justice, mercy, and solidarity that Jesus faced, we can see that that is the wrong response. The father affirms the special relationship that he has with the eldest. The eldest is heir to all that he has (v. 31); the father is not going to cast him out. Nevertheless it is right to celebrate the return of the lost. This story demonstrates the significance of the requirement to forgive "from the heart." No one is im-mune from the attitude expressed by the elder. But if such an attitude goes unchallenged it will divide the community. Sin-ners will always be "outcast." They will not really be restored as daughters and sons.

In other stories, the outcast sinner is contrasted with a Phar-isee who is confident in his own righteousness. A sinful wom-an anoints Jesus out of love and faith. Jesus' Pharisee host who protests is shown to be lacking in hospitality (Lk 7:36–50). The Pharisee who goes to pray in the Temple is further from God than the toll collector who acknowledges his sinfulness and seeks forgiveness (Lk 18:9–14). It is important to remember that Jesus does not reject the righteousness of people like the Pharisees or the elder son. But that righteousness remains im-perfect and divisive if it cannot see that God is now offering forgiveness to all.

Prayer and Our Relationship to God

We have already seen that our relationship to God in prayer and our relationship to others come together in the experience and

practice of forgiveness. Matthew 6:14–15 reiterates this petition from the Lord's Prayer (Mt 6:12). Forgiveness and prayer
are brought together in a saying of Jesus in Mark 11:25. The
exhortation to leave one's offering at the Temple altar and seek
reconciliation (Mt 5:23–4) shows the dramatic imagery so typical of Jesus. It suggests that someone who has not reconciled
with an offended party cannot expect to have his or her offering
accepted by God.

The Parable of the Toll Collector and the Pharisee serves as
an example of the Christian "prayer" in Luke. It contrasts a
Pharisee whose piety assures him that all is "right" between
himself and God with a tax collector who recognizes that he
has no claim on God's goodness. Christians are sometimes
accustomed to think of Pharisees as hypocritical in their devotion to God. Matthew 6:5–8 creates that impression by contrasting the behavior expected of Jesus' disciples with that of
"hypocrites" – a phrase used of the Pharisees. They pray extensively in public but have no true relationship with God. As a
result they are no better than the pagans who pray with lots of
words and formulas but to no avail, since they have no relationship with a real god. In the past, such passages have been
taken to justify disrespect or scorn for the worship of other
faiths. Today scholars recognize that their significance lies in a
different direction. The Christians in the communities for
which Matthew and Luke spoke had given up traditional, elaborate, and widely shared patterns of worship. Unlike some of
the mystery cults that were becoming popular in the gentile
world, Christians did not offer an alternative sacrificial priesthood, holy temple, and dramatic cult ritual. After the Temple
had been destroyed and Jewish Christians no longer partici-
pated in the life of local synagogues, they too had lost traditional forms of worship. Both groups may have wondered if
Christian prayer "on its own" was sufficient to maintain one's
relationship to God. The evangelists affirm that it is.

However, the move toward liturgical elaboration is evident in the Lord's Prayer (Mt 6:9–13//Lk 11:2–4). The opening of the prayer, addressed to God, resembles the Jewish Kaddish prayer: "Magnified and hallowed be His great name in the world which He created according to His will; and may He make His Kingship sovereign in your lifetime and in your days." Luke begins simply with the expression "Father." Matthew's version fills out the expression to create a parallel like the Jewish petition for the coming of the Kingdom. Matthew 6:10bc adds two phrases to that petition that spell out the significance of the Kingdom's coming. People will do the will of God with the same certainty that God's will is done in heaven. This expansion also balances the request that God act to make the coming of the Kingdom a reality with the three petitions that follow. As with the introduction, Matthew 6:13 balances the conclusion by adding a second clause. These changes have not altered the substance of the prayer, but have turned what might almost seem a telegraphic outline for prayer to God into a vehicle for communal prayer that Christians have used for millennia.

Most Christians substitute the "trespasses" (*paraptomata*) from Matthew 6:14 for the commercial metaphor of debt and debtor in Matthew 6:12. Luke 11:4 has an interesting combination of the two: God is asked to forgive our "sins" (*harmatiai*) as we forgive everyone indebted to us. This version of the prayer much more directly echoes the story of the unforgiving servant than Matthew's version. It raises the possibility that at some point in the tradition "forgiveness" did not refer simply to our relationship with persons who have done us an injury, but had a socioeconomic meaning. Instead of demanding collection on a debt, and perhaps reducing another to slavery in so doing, disciples should simply forgive what is owed. Such actions would destroy the relationships of dependence due to indebtedness and the various injustices associated with the system of legal regulations that created them.

The bread petition (Mt 6:11//Lk 11:3) points toward the teaching on anxiety (Mt 6:32–4; Lk 12:22, 30). The word "bread" is qualified by an unusual Greek expression, *epiousion*. Since ancient times there have been several guesses as to the meaning of that word: (1) If it is created from two Greek words, *epi* and *ousia* ("substance, being, essence"), it means "bread that is necessary for existence"; (2) if it comes from *epi* and *ousa* (present participle of the verb "to be"), and the word "day" is understood to be implied, it means "bread for the day"; (3) if it comes from *epi* and *iousa* (present participle of "to come"), again with "day" implied, it means "bread for the future" or the "coming day." Option (3) is often preferred by scholars who hold that the prayer refers to the eschatological banquet the disciples will celebrate with Jesus in the coming Kingdom (cf. Lk 13:29; 22:30). Options 1 and 2 are better suited to the petition as a reflection of Jesus' teaching about anxiety. Those who prefer option 2 point out that it may have been an allusion to the Greek translation of Exodus 16:4 in which the heavenly manna that the Israelites are instructed to gather only for a day is spoken of as "a day's portion for a day." The difficulty with both 2 and 3 is the necessity to supply "day" with the adjectival phrase without any indications of the need to do so in the text. Option 1 points directly toward the sayings about anxiety. It expresses confidence that the Lord will provide the disciples with what they need for survival.

The final petition acknowledges that the disciples live in a world where evil is still powerful. Jesus repeats this injunction as a caution to his disciples: "Pray that you do not enter into temptation" (Lk 22:40, 46). There the Lucan reader is shown an example of Jesus' own faithfulness in "testing" during the agony in Gethsemane. The Hebrew Scriptures describe God "testing" the faith of Israel (e.g., Ex 16:4; 20:20; Dt 8:2, 16; 13:5; 33:8). Exodus 16:4 makes a test of the requirement that Israel rely on God's daily manna from heaven: "whether they will walk in my Law or not." The prayer not to be brought to such a test also has echoes in the Psalms (e.g., 25:11; 51:5–6) and in another Jewish daily prayer: "Bring me not into sin nor into iniquity nor into temptation. And may the good inclination have sway over me and let not the evil inclination have sway over me." Matthew's addition, "rescue us from the Evil One," makes Satan the source of "testing" rather than God. Again, those who think the whole prayer is to be interpreted as a prayer for the coming of the Kingdom understand this "testing" to mean the final efforts of Satan to lead the righteous astray (e.g., Rv 3:10; Dn 12:10).

This tradition of eschatological "testing" is reflected in Mark 13:19–23, which states that the tribulations and Satanic deceit of the last days will be so bad that no one will be saved if God does not cut the time short! However, Luke's readers probably understood "testing" in a more general sense. If one looks back at Luke's rewriting of the interpretation of the Parable of the Sower (Lk 8:11–15; cf. Mk 4:14–20), one will notice that where Mark has "persecution" as the cause of some falling away, Luke has "temptation" (Lk 8:13). Luke expands the description of the "good" from hearing and accepting the word to include "hold it fast in an honest and good heart and bring forth fruit with patience" (Lk 8:15). For Luke's reader "temptation" might refer to anything that would cause a person to abandon Christianity rather than to endure in bringing forth good fruit.

For Luke Jesus exemplifies the importance of prayer. Not only does Jesus consistently withdraw to pray (e.g., Lk 6:12; 9:18; 22:39–41), he even prays words of obedience and confidence from the cross (23:46; cf. Ps 31:6). The Lord's Prayer is supplemented by other instruction on prayer. The Parable of the Persistent Friend (Lk 11:5–8) and sayings on the effectiveness of prayer (11:9–13) make it clear that one must also "endure" or persist in prayer. The Parable of the Unjust Judge is introduced as an example story for perseverance in prayer (18:1, 6). Much of this instruction emphasizes confidence in God. Christians can rely on the God they call "Abba" ("father") to sustain and provide for those who have put the Reign of God before everything else.

Love of One's Enemies

The various injunctions to love God, one's neighbor, and even one's enemies are among the most familiar parts of Jesus' teaching. Like much of Jesus' teaching, the idea that right-eousness, holiness, or wisdom manifests itself in "love" for the enemy is not unique. Jewish stories held up Joseph as a great example of someone who loved his enemies. Philosophers taught that the sage was above the passions of anger and re-taliation. The wise person would endure the insults or abuse of fools without replying in kind. Socrates repeatedly challenged the popular view that a "good" person tried to help friends and harm enemies.

Matthew's antithesis form in the Sermon on the Mount (Mt 5:43) might create the false impression that there was an in-junction to "hate one's enemies." Dualistic comments in some of the Essene writings that speak of the righteous "hating" the "children of darkness" are sometimes cited as parallels. How-ever, the Q version of the material on nonretaliation in Luke 6:27–36 opens not with a sharp contrast but with a list of parallel phrases that express the meaning of love of one's en-emies (vv. 27–8). Evidently Jesus' teaching on love of enemies was not expressed as a criticism of the Law or Jewish piety. These exhortations are framed as general statements of how the disciple responds to hostility.

Luke 6:29–30 gives particular instances of how a person would respond to concrete situations of conflict: a blow, sei-zure of one's cloak, beggars, someone who grabs what is yours.

Verse 31 concludes the section with another general statement: "Treat others as you wish them to treat you." Verses 32–6 present "love of enemies" in contrast to the behavior of "sinners" who also love those who love them. Luke has expanded the Q form of this section with the additional example of lending (vv. 34–5a) to create a triad of contrasting behaviors: love, help, and lend. This expansion provides another opportunity to emphasize the impact of Jesus' ethic on the rich. They must not simply lend with expectation of return. Even sinners know how to make money doing that. They must lend to those from whom they cannot expect anything. The conclusion of the section grounds the behavior in the example of God, who is also beneficent toward those who are ungrateful and wicked. The exhortation to imitate God's "mercy" (v. 36) may be an allusion to the command in Leviticus 19:2 to imitate God's holiness.

Matthew has divided the Q material in order to create two separate examples. The legal principle of appropriate retaliation rather than uncontrolled vengeance (Ex 21:23–5; Lv 24:19–20; Dt 19:21) forms the negative introduction to a section based on the concrete examples (Mt 5:38–42). As a result, Christians sometimes have a mistaken idea that the Law taught vengeance without mercy. Verse 39a provides the generalizing statement for the examples to replace the original "love your enemies." The examples are now illustrations of a principle: "Do not resist evil."

The examples are recast so that they express situations in which the hostility is expressed through social and legal gestures. The backhanded blow on the right cheek is not merely a shot in anger but a deliberate expression of contempt (v. 39b). One stands to lose one's cloak in a lawsuit. Instead of insisting that it be returned at night as specified in the Law (Ex 22:26–7; Dt 24:12–13; Am 2:8 condemns the rich for bedding down beside the altar in garments taken in pledge), one is to surrender one's tunic as well. Verse 41 adds a situation of enmity well known to people in an occupied territory as the land of Israel was: the possibility that an individual and/or his animals will be conscripted to carry persons or material. In order to prevent abuses, decrees might be posted that limited the extent to which such services could be demanded. Again, rather than insist on one's "rights," individuals are told to double the service they provide. In order to conclude the series with another institutionalized example of enmity, the original reference to begging is expanded with the example of lending (v. 42b).

Matthew's reworking of this material heightens its paradoxical character. The original examples might have referred simply to the everyday situations of conflict between individuals. The sayings would serve to stop hostilities at that level. These examples are more troubling because the evils that one is not to resist are institutionalized in the social and legal structure of the time. Is refusal to resist them and failure to take advantage of legal protections when they exist really the best way to ensure justice in a society?

Many Christians today would not agree with Matthew's understanding of this part of Jesus' teaching. They might argue that "not to resist evil" cannot be translated into passive cooperation with structures that contribute to it. Turning over a tunic as well as the cloak in which the poor person sleeps at night would simply encourage defrauding others in lawsuits, for example. Some scholars have answered this objection by arguing that these sayings are extreme examples designed to awaken our understanding of what it means to love one's enemy. They envisage relationships between persons that are not grounded on power, not even the claim to retribution for wrongs suffered.

The same emphasis on institutionalized violence is evident in Matthew's treatment of the sayings in the final section. The general experience of hostility becomes the specific case of reaction to the persecutor. (Thus Matthew recalls the righteous who suffer persecution for the Kingdom in vv. 10–12.) The motivating force of God's example occurs before the contrasting statements about human behavior. The reader is reminded that God causes the same sun to rise on the just and the unjust. This example has the tone of a proverbial wisdom saying and avoids directly claiming that God is "kind" to ingrates. The two examples of "love" among sinners have been recast from Q. The single category "sinner" has been divided into "toll collector" and "Gentile" (cf. the description of one expelled from the community in Mt 18:17) and the second behavior moderated to "greeting" one's fellows rather than helping them as in Q.

The final injunction asks the disciple to be "perfect" as God is rather than "merciful" as in Luke. Although it is difficult to be certain, Matthew would appear to be responsible for the shift. He introduces the injunction to the rich ruler who wants to be a disciple with, "If you would be perfect . . ." (19:21). "Perfect" appears occasionally in the Greek translation of the Hebrew Scriptures for "wholeness" as in Deuteronomy 18:13 or "blameless, pure" as in 2 Samuel 22:21–7. Essenes used the expression "perfect of way" for those who were wholeheartedly devoted to the community's understanding of the Law. Thus the expression "perfect" appears to encapsulate Matthew's understanding of discipleship for those whose righteousness exceeds that of scribes and Pharisees.

Matthew's focus on enmity created through persecution contains an important social consequence of "love of enemies." Blessing, praying for the persecutor, and not retaliating leave the door open to receive that person. A curse would imply formal exclusion, breaking off all relationships with the persecutor. Although Matthew's community is encouraged to see itself as distinctively different from the Jews and Gentiles of its environment, this identity is not reinforced by opposition to them.

One of the most striking examples of loving an enemy is in the Parable of the Good Samaritan (Lk 10:30–5), which we have already examined in another connection. Luke has inserted the parable into a discussion of love of God and neighbor as the epitome of the Law – a theme Luke took from Mark. The framework (vv. 29, 36–7) makes the parable an example story in a legal ruling over the extent of the word "neighbor." This ruling follows the spirit of Jesus' teaching on the extent of forgiveness in Matthew 18:21–2. It is essentially unlimited. Luke's reader has already been clued in to the hostile relationships between Samaritans and Jews when a Samaritan village refused Jesus and his disciples hospitality because they were pilgrims bound for Jerusalem (Luke 9:52–4). Jesus' own audience would certainly have shared the antipathy and even hatred toward the Samaritans typical of their time. They would have traveled the road Jesus asks them to imagine on pilgrimage to feasts in the Temple. After the priest and Levite had shunned the man, the hearer can hardly have expected much from a Samaritan. The story emphasizes the compassion shown by the Samaritan by giving extensive details of the actions he took in caring for the badly beaten man. He employs his material possessions to accomplish the task of caring for the man.

The example of the Good Samaritan shows the positive side of human relationships when the need of one person evokes the compassion and unselfish generosity of another. It does not resolve the "Jewish–Samaritan problem" on the political level. But as we have seen so often in the teaching of Jesus, people are not to remain imprisoned by the divisions that create antagonism and hostility. God's Reign belongs to all persons and requires no less than universal compassion.

Supplementary Reading and Discussion Questions

Additional information about topics, persons, and writings mentioned in the text can be found in general reference works such as Paul Achtemeier (ed.), *Harper's Bible Dictionary* (San Francisco: Harper & Row, 1985), and John Boardman, Jasper Griffin, and Oswyn Murray (eds.), *Oxford History of the Classical World* (Oxford: Oxford University Press, 1986).

Chapter 1

The authoritative history of this chapter's topic is H. I. Marrou, *A History of Education in Antiquity* (New York: New American Library, 1964). Readers interested in the role of the philosopher as moral educator told through representative selections from their writings should consult Abraham J. Malherbe, *Moral Exhortation: A Greco-Roman Sourcebook* (Philadelphia: Westminster, 1986). A general account of the role of scribes and Pharisees in Jewish society can be found in Anthony Saldarini, *Pharisees, Scribes and Sadducees in Palestinian Society* (Wilmington: Michael Glazier, 1988). A sourcebook that contains selections from Jewish writings and from the New Testament arranged according to themes is George Nickelsburg, *Faith and Piety in Early Judaism: Texts and Documents* (Philadelphia: Fortress, 1983).

1. How does Jesus compare with the four types of teacher common in antiquity – sage, philosopher, interpreter of the Law, prophet? What is the significance of the fact that Jesus did not found a school?

2. What is the role of conversion in a philosophical education? How would you compare that understanding of conversion with the prophetic call for repentance?
3. Describe the function of the Law of Moses as a moral educator. How is this role illustrated in Jewish traditions about Joseph?

Chapter 2

A recent popular work that seeks to use archaeological evidence to situate Jesus within Judaism of his time is James H. Charlesworth, *Jesus within Judaism* (Garden City, N.Y.: Doubleday, 1988). Two studies that are more attentive to the scholarly difficulties of recovering the teaching of the historical Jesus are Norman Perrin, *Rediscovering the Teaching of Jesus* (New York: Harper & Row, 1967), and E. P. Sanders, *Jesus and Judaism* (Philadelphia: Fortress, 1985). An important study of the place of women in Jesus' ministry is Ben Witherington, *Women in the Ministry of Jesus* (Cambridge: Cambridge University Press, 1984).

1. What do we mean when we speak of Jesus as a charismatic figure? How do the gospel writers establish this picture of Jesus in narrating Jesus' "call" and in depicting the responses of others to him?
2. What demands does Jesus make on those who wish to become his disciples? Why would these demands have shocked people in his time?
3. How are women portrayed in the Gospels as followers of Jesus? What is the social significance of Jesus reaching out to women and children?

Chapter 3

A description of the style of Jesus' teaching that contrasts the Marcan account with stories about philosophers and ancient rhetorical practice is Vernon K. Robbins, *Jesus the Teacher: A Socio-rhetorical Interpretation of Mark* (Philadelphia: Fortress, 1984). A different approach, based on formalist literary criticism, seeks to show how Jesus' teaching breaks apart our expectations about reality: See Bernard Brandon Scott, *Jesus, Symbol-Maker for the Kingdom* (Philadelphia: Fortress, 1981). Scott has carried this approach further in his commentary on the parables, *Hear Then the Parable: A Commentary on the Parables of Jesus* (Minneapolis: Fortress, 1989). For a treatment of the parables of Jesus that focuses on their human and religious message see Pheme Perkins, *Hearing the Parables of Jesus* (Mahwah, N.J.: Paulist, 1981). An extensive account of the background to and use of the expression "Kingdom of God" can be found in G. R. Beasley-Murray, *Jesus and the Kingdom of God* (Grand Rapids, Mich.: Eerdmans, 1986).

1. Describe the characteristics of proverbs, parables, legal sayings, and prophetic or apocalyptic sayings. How does Jesus use exaggeration to capture the imagination of the audience in each type of saying?

2. Audience responses to the parables of Jesus would have differed depending on assumptions made about the subject matter, evaluation of the behavior of characters in the parable, and the social, economic, or religious background of the hearer. Explain how these different responses are illustrated in the Parable of the Sower. Then suggest diverse responses for one of the other narrative parables such as the Good Samaritan or the Prodigal Son.

3. What are the characteristics of the Reign (Kingdom) of God in the teaching of Jesus? How does Jesus challenge the views of his contemporaries about God's Rule?

Chapter 4

An excellent account of the picture of Jesus in the synoptic Gospels and Q can be found in Jack D. Kingsbury, *Jesus Christ in Matthew, Mark, and Luke* (Philadelphia: Fortress, 1981). John D. Donahue, *The Gospel in Parable* (Philadelphia: Fortress, 1988), shows how the parables fit into the theology of each of the evangelists. Two detailed treatments of the Sermon on the Mount that show readers the process and results of scholarly analysis are Jan Lambrecht, *The Sermon on the Mount: Proclamation and Exhortation* (Wilmington: Michael Glazier, 1985), and Georg Strecker, *The Sermon on the Mount* (Nashville: Abingdon, 1988).

1. What beliefs about Jesus made him different from other famous teachers of his time? How do these beliefs influence the way in which the Gospel writers adapt Jesus traditions to their own times?

2. Describe form criticism, source criticism, and redaction criticism. How are insights from each of these methods of analysis used to help us understand Jesus' teaching about divorce as it is presented in the Gospels?

3. What are the characteristics of true ("higher") righteousness in Matthew? How does Matthew use the literary device of drawing sharp contrasts between the disciples of Jesus and others to emphasize these characteristics?

Chapter 5

In addition to the books on the parables and the Sermon on the Mount referred to in the bibliographies to Chapters 3 and 4, see Pheme Perkins, *Love Commands in the New Testament* (Mahwah, N.J.: Paulist, 1982). For an account of the traditions of justice and solidarity with the poor in Jesus' teaching, Q, and Luke that reflects the concerns of liberation theology see Luise Schottroff and Wolfgang Stegemann, *Jesus and the Hope of the Poor* (Maryknoll, N.Y.: Orbis, 1986).

1. Describe Jesus' vision of justice for the poor and oppressed. How is the gospel message "good news" for those groups?

2. How do the petitions of the Lord's Prayer describe the life of Christian discipleship? What is the relationship between forgiveness and prayer in the life of the disciple?

3. Give examples of Jesus' teaching on love of enemies. How do these examples address problems of violence and evil in human relationships?

Index

109

112 Index